With her mother in hospital ~~~~~~~ small village that couldn't b~~~~~~~~~~~~~~~~~~~~~~ed. For a start, the villagers kn~~~~~~~~~~~~ about each other and the village school is nothing like the private school she has just left. On top of all this, when Helen does go back to London in September, she'll be starting at the local comprehensive.

So this summer term at the village school is going to be like the filling in a sandwich – between Craddock House at Easter and the comprehensive in the autumn. The big question is, what's it going to taste like?

At first it's as bad as she ever imagined, with people tormenting her and sneering at the way she speaks. But then she finds her feet, makes some unexpected friends and does some much-needed growing up.

Readers of ten and over will recognize Helen's problems and enjoy this modern school story.

TIM KENNEMORE

➤ ❋ ❋ ➤

The Middle of the Sandwich

PUFFIN BOOKS

IN ASSOCIATION WITH FABER & FABER

Puffin Books, Penguin Books Ltd, Harmondsworth, Middlesex, England
Penguin Books, 625 Madison Avenue, New York, New York 10022, U.S.A.
Penguin Books Australia Ltd, Ringwood, Victoria, Australia
Penguin Books Canada Ltd, 2801 John Street, Markham, Ontario, Canada L3R 1B4
Penguin Books (N.Z.) Ltd, 182–190 Wairau Road, Auckland 10, New Zealand

First published by Faber & Faber Limited 1981
Published in Puffin Books 1983

Made and printed in Great Britain by
Cox & Wyman Ltd, Reading
Set in Sabon

Chapter One

→ ❈ ❈ ←

HELEN WAS WRITING to her mother, and there was nothing to say. She peeked over the top of her Muppet writing-pad at Jess. Her aunt, sitting at the kitchen table, was doing fascinating things with a large, pinkish sheet of cardboard, ruler, pencil and black felt tip. All much more interesting than letter-writing. Helen sighed and gazed at Kermit as if hoping for inspiration, but Kermit just stared back, green and indifferent.

Jess ruled another line. "What on earth can you think of to write about? You only left her yesterday. Wait till school starts."

"But that's not till *Tuesday*. She goes into hospital on Tuesday. And I promised to write *often*."

"Whatever you say." Jess transferred her attention back to the cardboard. Helen's curiosity finally got the better of her.

"Are you doing something for school?"

"New Team List. Last term the Robins came bottom every week, and the Sparrows came top. Everyone except the Sparrows got bored with it. I'm trying to get them more balanced. Not easy."

Helen went to look over her aunt's shoulder.

"How many teams do you have? How many children? What do they come top and bottom in?"

Jess took the questions in reverse order, in Miss-World-announcing style.

"Good marks and stars during the week, added up; points knocked off for bad behaviour, lateness, and assorted crimes too horrible to mention. Thirty-nine Infants. Four teams."

"Ten a side, with one missing."

"That's it. So I put a couple of brighter sparks into the team with one short. Only last term the sparks were too bright, and, as I said, they won every week. That's what I'm trying to get right now."

"Does Mrs. Page have teams too?"

"Certainly. Only hers seem to balance better than mine do. Let's see, she's got thirty-two at the moment. You'll make thirty-three. I wonder where she'll put you. Depends whether she thinks you'll be a credit or a liability."

This, at the moment, was the least of Helen's worries. Only a fortnight ago she'd been told, out of the blue, that her mother was to have a serious operation, and that she, Helen, would have to go and stay with Jess in deepest Essex, and join Jess's school for the summer term. And, even worse, she would *never* return to Craddock House, her old school, because she was thirteen, and in the autumn she'd be starting at the Comprehensive, back home in Wimbledon. There hadn't even been time for Helen to say good-bye. The Comprehensive was a horrendous thought, but it wasn't going to happen until September, which looked at from March was far enough ahead not to get panicky about, yet. West Haysham Combined School, a sudden world of strangers, had been totally unexpected, and Helen was scared stiff.

"Well," Jess said, "I ought to be thinking about tea. How would sausages and chips grab you?"

Helen thought that sausages and chips would grab her very pleasantly, whatever her mother said about fried foods bringing on an untimely death, and was promptly sent out to buy cooking oil. It was quite a relief to get away. She was not comfortable with Jess, partly because she was never certain if her aunt was laughing at her, and partly because she was still shy. She had known Jess all her life as a pleasant if rather remote aunt, but she had never known her well. She and Mum would see Jess perhaps twice a year, occasionally stay with her for a few days, but Jess and Helen had never been left alone before, without Mum, sister of one and mother of the other, to bridge the gap.

West Haysham lay still and quiet, a subdued country village, all dull browns, greens and greys, nothing bright or eye-catching. There was a family legend that once, when Helen had just started toddling, she had toddled off down the road into a still-steaming pile of horse manure, fallen full-length on top of it, and been carried off, screaming with fury. She'd heard this often enough to be unsure whether she actually remembered it or only *thought* she did, but at this moment Helen felt certain that the incident had happened, just as they told it, and that every single person in the village knew about it. She would not have been surprised to find faces watching from behind twitching curtains, hoping that she might do it again.

The silence of the village hit her like a blast of cold air. It was like a television with the sound turned down; like being in a world which needs a new set of batteries. London, with its busy streets throbbing with traffic, people, life, could have been on another planet. Here, the single bird that began to chirrup overhead was deafening.

Between Jess's house and the shops was the village pub, the Fountain; a chubby, pig-faced girl was swooping up and down in a swing in the Children's Garden. Her dress was far too short, and, during the upward phase of her swing, her navy-blue knickers were clearly visible, between her fat little pink legs. It was a horrible sight.

"What are you staring at?"

Taken aback, Helen almost said, "your knickers", stopped just in time, and, casting about frantically in her mind for an acceptable answer, finally produced:

"The swing. I wish I had one," she added lamely, cross that her voice had gone hoarse and cracked as it always did when she was nervous. The girl appeared satisfied with this answer.

"Are you Miss Cottis's niece, then?"

"That's right," croaked Helen. "Sorry, but I have to hurry . . ." *Fool*, she told herself fiercely, once she was well past the pub. You should have stopped to talk, then you might *know* somebody on Tuesday . . .

She tried her voice, softly, to see if it had returned to normal, which, of course, it had, now that nobody was listening. Helen's mother had a theory that a London accent would be a handicap in later years, and had sent her to Craddock House, to 'mix with the right type of child'. Mum was very fussy about her speech, for ever correcting it – 'It's different *from*, not different *to* . . . Deborah and I, not me and Deborah' – sometimes Helen was stopped so often in mid-speech that she lost all track of what she'd been saying. It seemed almost as if her mother wasn't interested in what she said – only that she said it properly.

The largest of the shops, a mini-mini-supermarket, looked a likely bet for the cooking oil; Helen bought it, and was just about to cross the road when a car slowed down and jerked to a stop by her side.

"Someone's going to ask me the way to somewhere," she thought at once. "They always do when you don't know." The driver, a woman, leaned over and rolled down the window, poking out a long, lean face.

"Would you be Helen? Jess Cottis's niece?" Helen agreed to this. It sounded as if Jess had been walking the streets with a loud-speaker, announcing her imminent arrival. She waited for the woman to say something about the manure.

"I've been hoping to see you." The woman had a dazzling smile—her teeth gleamed white, one could almost imagine them being used as emergency fog lamps. "I was going to call round. Needn't bother now. We'd very much like you to come to tea with us, get acquainted. Which day would suit you best? We're going out on Saturday ... Friday? Or Sunday?"

"Either would be lovely," Helen said, wishing she knew who the woman was, but not liking to ask. She scuffed the pavement nervously with her right foot. The woman looked down at it. The foot, as if mesmerised, was instantly still.

"Let's make it Sunday, then, give you time to draw breath. About three? Tell Jess I'll bring you back in the car and drop off the veg. at the same time. We'll be looking forward to seeing you." With a slight cough, the car, a red Mini, pulled away.

I've been ages, Helen thought guiltily as she scampered up Jess's path. Mum would have been flapping by now, in case Helen had been reduced to strawberry jam by a hit-and-run driver, or abducted by a passing child-molester. Jess, however, chips chipped and sausages gently spluttering, was placidly mashing a tin of food for her cat, Logan.

9

"I'm sorry I was so long." Helen took out the cooking oil. "You weren't worrying, were you?"

Jess glanced at the clock.

"You've been exactly twenty-two minutes. I didn't think it necessary to call the Yard in, just yet. All right, you." This to Logan, who was perched on the table, lovingly rubbing his head against her. She put the bowl down; the cat leapt off the table and ran to it, purring.

"Cupboard lover," Jess said, with affection. She didn't seem surprised to hear about the woman in the Mini. "That's Mrs. Pargeter. She told me she'd like to have you round. You'll be seeing a lot of her, she helps with games at the school. Amazing energy, that woman. She's on umpteen committees, including the Provisional Committee to Save Our School, of which she's the Provisional Head..."

"Save it from what?"

"Closing down. We've been expecting it for years—they've been axing small schools all over the country, and schools don't come a lot smaller than ours. Nothing's been said yet, but we're determined to keep a step ahead. Hence the Provisional Committee. We can mobilise for battle in no time. Now I've side-tracked myself. What was I saying?"

"About Mrs. Pargeter."

"Oh yes. Well, they grow vegetables for half the village, and she plays golf—she used to be a magistrate, but all that and bringing the boys up was too much even for her, so she gave it up when the fifth one came along..."

"The *fifth*?" Helen was aghast. "Five boys, and she's asked me to tea? Five boys won't want a girl coming. It'll be terrible. They won't know what to do with me."

"Try not to be sillier than you can help," Jess said, not unkindly. "The Pargeters are the nicest boys I know, and I

10

ought to know, since I've taught two of them, and am currently teaching another two. And as Jonathan's not eighteen months yet he's not likely to trouble you much, one way or the other. So let's have no more nonsense."

That seemed to be that; Helen took her plate, poured a splodge of tomato sauce, spun the plate round until the sauce was exactly at four o'clock, where she liked it, and began to eat, watching with surprise as Jess dished out a good-sized helping for herself. Somehow she hadn't expected this; after years of her mother's diets she'd got into the habit of thinking that grown-ups mostly lived on lettuce and cottage cheese.

Chapter Two

THE GIRL ON THE swing had a friend round today—they were sitting giggling over a magazine. Helen hurried past, hoping not to be noticed. Jess had identified the girl as Beverley Simmons, daughter of the pub's landlord. Helen had never before known a Beverley; it immediately became a fat, pudgy-faced name.

Three o'clock on Sunday had drawn inexorably closer, casting a gloomy shadow over the whole weekend. By half-past two Helen had realized that she was not actually going to be sick, however much she might feel like it, and was perched on a kitchen chair, drumming her fingers on the table and rehearsing bright, intelligent things to say to the Pargeters.

"You've hardly eaten a thing all day," Jess said, watching her. "What's there to be so scared of?"

Helen could not begin to explain. The boys at Craddock House had been a thing apart; girls and boys, while occupying the same rooms, had treated each other with great scorn. Mixing on equal terms, making friends, had been out of the question, and yet she was expected to do so this afternoon. Jess shook her head.

"I'd go now, if I were you. If you sit there thinking about

it much longer you'll work yourself up till you're ill."
Helen sighed—if she had known this was possible she
would have sat there, thinking about it, ever since Thursday. The accumulation of all that thought should have
been enough to have her flat on her back for a week.

Long Acre, the Pargeter house, was large and white,
with a bow window spilling out on to the front lawn. A
thick-set man was painting window-frames, looking
alarmingly top-heavy on a spindly ladder. Mr. Pargeter.

"You'll be Helen? They're all round the back. Go
straight through." Helen followed the path round and
emerged on to a great length of garden. Pargeters were
scattered everywhere. Mrs. Pargeter, some distance away,
was bent over a vegetable bed; seeing Helen, she waved,
straightened and walked over, lithe and graceful.

Helen already knew the Pargeter boys from Jess's de-
scriptions. Richard, the eldest, and Andrew, the brainy
one, were playing badminton, using a rope as a net. Next
came Michael, who was charging up and down with a
bow and arrows. Michael was beautiful. Alex, angel-fair,
thin and ethereal, had a friend over to play. This outsider
was quite clearly that; he was far too plain to belong to the
good-looking Pargeters. The baby, Jonathan, was crouch-
ing over a battered wooden truck, intent on some secret
game.

Helen only just managed to keep her voice from crack-
ing as she said hello, and Mrs. Pargeter, who knew a
nervous child when she saw one, said briskly:

"Andrew, go and find another racket, and you can play
two against one for a while." Thankfully, this meant that
there was no further need for talk except for shouts of
"Good shot" and Andrew calling "Mine" and "Yours".
Once Helen had stopped expecting the shuttlecock to
bounce she rapidly got the hang of the game, gained confi-

dence and, almost without noticing, began calling back to Andrew. It was impossible to concentrate and still remember to be shy. Mrs. Pargeter smiled secretly at a cauliflower.

"Anyone want some Coke?" she called after a while. The scattered children, attracted by the magic word 'Coke' as by the Pied Piper's music, immediately converged on the garden table. Michael appeared from the front of the house, minus bow and arrows.

"I hope you haven't been frightening the Wilkes sisters with those things, Robin Hood," his mother told him sternly, putting down a large tray. "No, Jon, you come with me and you shall have orange squash in your special cup. Biscuit, Helen?"

"Yes, please." Helen had somehow lost her nervous tension without even being aware of it. These Pargeters were so comfortable to be with, not asking all the time if she was enjoying herself—they were just right. They didn't ignore her, but they didn't try too hard, either.

Once she had stopped trying to sound bright, and being self-conscious about it, her voice became quite natural and soon she was chatting with the others, except for Alex's friend Mark, who sat, still and speechless as the Sphinx, sucking his straw. And, as usual, once she was contented, wanting the afternoon to drag by, time flew. They watched a television serial, which was a pleasant change—Jess didn't have a television—and before she knew it tea was ready.

Truly hungry after her earlier perfunctory meals, Helen was able to do justice to the lavish spread in far better fashion than her normal rather small appetite would have allowed, which was very gratifying to Mrs. Pargeter.

"What year are you in?" Richard asked. "How old are you?"

14

"Thirteen last month. I was in the last year at middle school."

"Older than me!" He looked somewhat taken aback.

"In these remote parts we make do with a junior and middle school rolled into one," his mother said. "You'll be in the top group, of course."

"Paul *will* be pleased," said Andrew. This caused great amusement.

"Paul has been on his own with four girls all the way up the school," explained Mrs. Pargeter. "He puts up with it very well, poor chap."

"You'll be with Joanne and Lorraine," said Richard, "and Melanie, and Beverley Simmons..." Michael let out a howl of disgust at the words 'Beverley Simmons'

Helen was surprised at the amount of difference between the Pargeters. She was accustomed to thinking of boys as an undistinguishable mass; now she saw that even when they were brothers they could vary greatly. Richard had considerable presence—tall, composed, very much the older brother. Andrew was much paler, a shadow; like many bespectacled young boys he had the look of a budding nuclear scientist or brain surgeon. Michael was totally different again—a jumping jack, a banger, behind that amazing face, every feature quite perfect.

She scarcely noticed the two youngest. Jonathan took little interest in anything but food and his truck. Alex looked fragile and breakable enough to crack into pieces at any moment; he was very self-possessed and most unchildlike, with a high, piercing voice. Alex was a pale yellow person.

She could never help thinking of people as colours. It was as if an aura of a particular shade floated about their heads, visible only to Helen's imagination. Richard was mid-blue, very cool, rather superior; Andrew light green,

15

less important, not a primary colour. Michael was bright scarlet, zappy, fiery. Her mother varied between rust-brown and orange, depending on her mood. With Mum, a lot depended on her mood. Jess was jet black, very rare and vaguely alarming. About herself Helen was never sure. Trying to picture herself from the outside, as other people saw her, conjured up no colour at all, just a nothingness, like the nothing-colour of her hair.

"She's miles away," she heard Andrew say.

"Oh, I'm sorry . . . were you talking to me?"

"Thinking at the table is not a capital offence," Mrs. Pargeter said, buttering a piece of bread for Jonathan. "We'll let you live, this time."

"But only if you tell us *exactly* what you were thinking about," Richard said. "Otherwise Mum'll put you through the mincer and bury you in the garden to fertilise the cabbages."

"I was just thinking what a boring colour my hair is." It sounded so silly and girlish, unless you knew the reasoning behind it, but she had no intention of going into that. She waited to be laughed at. The boys, however, took her answer seriously.

"Same colour as Mum's," said Alex. "What colour do you call your hair, Mum?" With his precise little voice he was like a miniaturised adult. The single crumb on his left cheek looked ridiculously out of place. "I know what it's like," he went on, without waiting for an answer. He found the offending crumb and flicked it away delicately with the edge of a napkin. "Porridge."

"Thank you very *much*," said his mother. "For that, you can have a piece of Helen's hair for breakfast tomorrow."

Helen had a strong suspicion that Alex was not going to be her favourite Pargeter.

Tea finished, she was taken upstairs for a guided tour of the boys' books, toys, games and models, champion among which was Richard's *Cutty Sark*, truly magnificent, surrounded by an armada of smaller craft. "Excuse the mess," Mrs. Pargeter called up. "We only got back from France on Tuesday." Richard explained that they stayed with an aunt in Marseilles every Easter.

"I *thought* you were rather brown for the time of year."

"Except Alex. If he stays in the sun he goes bright red like a beetroot and starts peeling round the edges." Helen said nothing; a red, peeled Alex might look human, which would be a definite improvement.

She was surprised at the easy way in which the Pargeters had accepted her as a guest. Perhaps when there were five children already, one extra here or there didn't make much difference. She was quite cross when Mrs. Pargeter interrupted the third re-run of the Monaco Grand Prix, being run on a very superior four-car racing set, to say that it was about time she took Helen home.

"Richard and Andrew, come down and help me load the car . . . Alex, you should have been in bed half an hour ago."

"Don't forget to cut some hair for his breakfast," Michael said, shooting his car into the pits for repairs.

"Bed for you too, young man, the moment I get back."

"That was stupid," Richard said. "You shouldn't have reminded her you were there."

Mr. Pargeter, looming even larger at ground level, was polishing golf clubs. He stood up and solemnly shook Helen's hand.

"You must think I'm a shocking host, young lady."

Helen made negative noises. On the whole she'd been rather relieved that he'd kept out of the way.

"Still, I expect we'll be seeing you again, if you haven't

been put off by my horde of backward yobs." Helen thought this rather hard; as boys went, Mr. Pargeter had fairly good specimens, and certainly not backward, but a grinning Andrew explained that 'backward yob' was just a Pargeter way of saying 'boy'.

The back seat of the Mini was buried beneath boxes of Pargeter produce, and, mysteriously, a number of empty bottles, which rattled ominously as Mrs. Pargeter slid into first gear.

"When is your mother having the operation?" she asked, sympathetically.

"Wednesday." *Wednesday!* Only two more days and they'd be cutting Mum up. Oh, horrors. She had a flashing vision of a surgeon wielding a long, sharp, wicked-looking knife, pints of blood bucketing on to the floor . . . how had Wednesday managed to creep so close, without her noticing?

Jess, hearing the car, came out to meet them.

"I see your boys didn't eat her for tea. She rather thought they might."

"Heavens, no. I think they got on very well." Helen loathed being discussed like this, in her hearing, but could see no way to escape without being rude.

"I can't imagine that she's been much trouble."

"Quiet as a mouse," Mrs. Pargeter beamed. Desperate to stop this, Helen risked interrupting with: "Thank you for having me, Mrs. Pargeter."

"It was a pleasure," Mrs. Pargeter said, predictably, and led Jess to the car. "Still a bit early in the year, but I've cut you a fair bit of purple sprouting, there's rhubarb, a nice cauli . . ." Helen, obediently ferrying bottles into the hall, was further confused to find more bottles, full ones, standing in a tidy line against the wall, as if queueing for a bus.

18

"Ten green bottles, standing in the hall," said Helen.

"Moonshine," Jess said. "And if one green bottle should accidentally fall, Dorothy, you'll arrive home with a lot of broken glass and a nasty stained car. I'll find a box." Of course—Jess made wine. Helen could dimly recall her turning up on her rare London visits with bottles for Mum to sample, and Mum, later, throwing them away, because she didn't trust home-made wine at all.

Mrs. Pargeter and Jess disappeared outside, and Helen skipped upstairs to the lavatory, nearly falling over Logan who, like Kermit's little nephew Robin, liked to sit not at the bottom, not at the top, but exactly half-way down the stairs.

Chapter Three

"WELL, YOU SEEM TO have made a fair impression," Jess said, closing the back door. "You're invited to go to the seaside with them when the weather improves, so they can't actually have hated you."

Helen realized she was being teased. "I didn't actually hate them either. They aren't at all like the boys at my other school."

"What did you do?"

"We watched *Treasure Island*..."

"Message received loud and clear. Television. Don't tell me you're getting withdrawal symptoms."

"Like Mum, every time she gives up smoking? No, I don't really miss it all that much. It isn't—isn't *needed* here, you're always doing something. Mum doesn't. She says she needs the TV in the evenings to relax her after working all day. She has it on all night. It's quite peaceful without."

"*Does* she? Good Lord. My sister, the television addict." Jess was pouring coffee. "Want some?" Helen shook her head. "And what do you do all evening, while Barbara's glued to the box?"

"Well, I do watch Top of the Pops, things like that, then there's homework—sometimes I go round to Deborah's, or she comes to us. Or I do a jigsaw, or read. I read a lot."

"You haven't done much reading here."

"Only brought one book. I finished that Thursday night in bed."

"Good heavens, why didn't you ask? I could have found you something ... never mind, you can have the pick of our school library. Tell me, does your mother never go out, or have friends round?"

Helen considered. "Friends, sometimes. The main one was Alison until she moved. You know her, she's the one Mum's going to stay with to con ... con ..."

"Convalesce."

"Convalesce. She doesn't like me, that Alison. She doesn't like any children."

"Sounds as if that's mutual. Go on."

"Well, most of her other friends are work friends. She comes to school things, and we go out at weekends. Other than that, not much, I suppose. It's because of when I was little, she didn't really trust baby-sitters, she says."

"And she's got out of the habit. I know," Jess said, sipping coffee thoughtfully. "Not much life for a young woman. She's not much over thirty. It's a shame that she never married again. No, don't look at me like that, Helen. You're quite old enough to realize that people do re-marry, especially when they're widowed so young. It's a struggle, bringing up a child on your own, even with a good job. And she was determined that you should go to a private school till you were thirteen. She must have sacrificed a lot for that."

"I wouldn't have minded going to an ordinary school," Helen said, feeling some self-defence to be called for.

"No, but that's not really the point. The right sort of stepfather would probably have been a very good thing for you."

21

This was a completely unexplored line of thought. Mum married, Mrs. Something-Else. A stepfather. It seemed unlikely. The only candidate she could think of was Mr. Cochrane at work, who had already been married three times and had seven children. Mum had shown little desire to become the fourth Mrs. Cochrane.

"But, Aunt Jess, you've never married even once," she ventured, not sure if this was cheek. Jess appeared undisturbed.

"Your mother and I are two very different people. She's the marrying kind, white wedding at nineteen, blissfully happy. I'm not. Marriage means compromise, you know—adapting to another person. I'd have resented that. I like to do things my way." She smiled at her niece. "Do you understand?"

"Yes, I think so. It's strange, I never really thought about what you were like before. I just thought of you as an older Mum. But you're not. You're quite different."

"As different as two sisters can be," agreed Jess. "Heavens, all this deep talk. It's quarter to nine. Do you fancy you could carry a full demijohn upstairs without disaster?"

"Those?" Helen pointed at the two large, narrow-necked glass jars which stood in the corner. "I fancy I could. As long as Logan isn't on his stair."

"Date wine," Jess said, nodding at the deep gold liquid. "Did it while you were out."

"*Dates?* What else do you make wine from?" Helen asked, beginning the ascent with concentration.

"All sorts. Carrots, parsnips, bananas, berries—you'd be surprised what goes into some of them. So would the people who drink it. I never put the ingredients on the label. I call them Light Table Wine, Port, Dry Sherry... We have a private village barter system. The Pargeters, for

22

instance—they provide me with garden produce, I give them my deadly potions. That rhubarb you've been eyeing so unenthusiastically will make a very nice table wine."

It occurred to Helen that Jess, with her black cat and her potions, was like a sort of modern-day witch. "Where now?" she asked, reaching the landing, demijohn hugged close to her chest.

"Airing cupboard." The airing cupboard was lined with demijohns wall to wall; a few sheets, looking out of place, had been relegated to the back of a shelf. Helen was fascinated by the rows of brews, some of which were actually bubbling; she turned away reluctantly.

"I suppose I ought to go to bed?"

"Tired?"

"No, not a bit. But, you know, nine o'clock . . ."

"I'm sure Barbara allows you an occasional extension. Why not live riotously for once, and stay up till ten? I'll teach you backgammon."

"Is that the funny board with triangles? Isn't it very difficult?"

"Helen, you must try to be aware of your possibilities as well as your limitations," said Jess in a teacherly voice. "If you can count up to twelve, and I have every confidence that you can do that, you can play backgammon. Come along."

Helen went.

"Well?" said Jess over the top of her *Daily Telegraph*. "Dead on your feet after finally staggering to bed at ten-thirty?"

Helen giggled, sinking into a chair. "I think I'll live. I never go to sleep straight away anyhow. I nearly always hear the end music of News at Ten."

"Then what's the point of . . . oh well." Jess looked as if she could have said a lot more. "Breakfast?"

Jess was not a breakfast-eater herself, and had stocked her cupboard with four different brands of cereal for Helen's benefit. To combat the monotony of this Helen had adapted the system of rotating crops, remembered from history lessons, for her own purposes, using a Cereal Rotation System. She now mentally reviewed this.

"Rice Krispies, please." After Jess had gone to such trouble, she didn't like to say that she would actually much prefer toast and peanut butter.

Jess doled out cereal. "I'll be going over to the school, later on. You're welcome to come and lend a hand, meet Mrs. Page."

This was clearly a good offer. It would be a distinct advantage to have advance knowledge of the school's layout, not to mention Mrs. Page. Helen had come to think of her school career as a giant sandwich. Craddock House, behind her, and the Comprehensive, still ahead, were the two thick slices of bread; the single term at West Haysham was the filling. It might turn out to be delicious, like peanut butter, or something she hated, like fish paste. She'd get her first nibble of the sandwich tomorrow.

The school, solid stone in its concrete playground, was less than five minutes' walk from Jess's front door. "This is the Infants' cloakroom," Jess said, waving her rolled-up Team List. "Through here, Infants' room. That"—she pointed disdainfully—"is what Mrs. Page and I laughingly call our office. Also used as dishing-out-lunchery, dentistry, anything elsery . . ."

"And this is what we laughingly call Mrs. Page," said Helen's new form teacher, appearing at the far end of the room. "Hello, Helen." She was a sturdy, sensible-looking sort of woman, fifty or so, a striking contrast with slim, dark Jess, who must be at least forty but looked ten years younger.

The teachers exchanged pleasantries about the holidays, which Mrs. Page had spent in her native Yorkshire. Her accent was not strong, but it could be detected, very slightly Michael Parkinson.

Helen gazed around in wonderment. No desks—tables, pushed together into blocks; lofty ceiling, arched in the middle, disappearing skyward; white-painted walls, bright posters, last term's Team List. In this one room you could have fitted two Craddock House formrooms, desks with antiquated inkwells arranged in tidy rows.

Mrs. Page took her through to the Juniors' room. This was smaller, with large windows set high in the wall. The Juniors, clearly, were not intended to admire the view.

"Lovely view of the golf course if you happen to be seven foot six," said Mrs. Page. "There's the top group table. We invade the Infants every morning for Assembly, and again for lunch. Now, you could start changing the posters. Take down Coal Mining, that's none too inspiring, and Dwellings Through the Ages can go too; if I look at that Roman Villa much longer I'll go mad."

Helen, deciding tentatively that she was *probably* going to like Mrs. Page, and, though shy, not uncomfortably so, scrambled on to a chair and began removing drawing pins. The new posters were all about Australia: a map, Sheep Farming, Wildlife.

"There's a good series on this term. The Smallest Continent."

"Oh, you mean Schools Programmes on TV? I've never seen those before."

"I think you'll enjoy them. We watch quite a number, and they're a lot better than the junk I sometimes see in the evenings. The Bionic Woman! The Six Million Dollar

Man!" She said this with great disgust; Helen wondered what bionics had done to Mrs. Page, that she should dislike them so. It would be interesting to see her reaction to the Incredible Hulk. "I must be getting out of touch," she went on. "They can't decide whether to have me condemned or to preserve me as an Ancient Monument. I was talking to my niece in Halifax—she's fifteen—she says I ought to be presented to the British Museum."

Helen, who had been listening with mounting fascination, wondered if she would ever dare to say such a thing to Jess, and thought it unlikely. She gazed at the Aborigine Boy who was glaring at her malevolently, spear in hand, from a corner of one of the posters, decided she disliked him and stuck a drawing pin through his right eyeball.

Finally emerging from her desk drawers, Mrs. Page flipped the calendar over to April. "Now, if I'm not mistaken, that's your aunt boiling the kettle for coffee."

Jess was. "I told Helen she could take some books out today, if that's all right with you."

"Of course. I'll do her tickets, she'll be needing them."

Helen sat on the floor in front of the three shelves of books that comprised the Junior Library, and passed an enjoyable five minutes choosing. Mrs. Page slotted the cards into her tickets. "We have library once a week. Joanne and Lorraine are the librarians. Have you met them? No. I'll introduce you tomorrow." She went on to enquire, with concern, about Helen's mother.

"She's phoning me here from the hospital tomorrow," said Jess, "and I'll ring from here on Wednesday, after the op."

Helen, who had been luxuriating in the strange sensation of being the only child in school, was once again taken aback by the very nearness of the operation. It was hardly believable—Mum, seeing her off five days earlier, had looked so normal, so unneeding of surgery. There was something, at the back of her mind, so dreadful that she was scared to think about it properly. Mum might die. People *did* die, in operations. And only a week ago she had read of a girl who had suffered permanent brain damage, had been turned into a vegetable, by being given the wrong gas during an operation. It was too frightening to contemplate. Mum, reading the same article later, had paled and turned the page very fast.

"You've never had this operation, have you, Aunt Jess?" she asked later, back home.

"Of course not. It's not *that* common...." Jess wheeled round from the cooker and gazed searchingly at her niece. "Helen, I've deliberately kept off the subject, but it seems to be bothering you—do you know exactly what the operation is?"

Helen shook her head. "Mum calls it ladies' trouble, what she's had." It had all been very puzzling. Mum had not seemed ill in the way Helen understood it: lying in bed, doctor visiting, medicines prescribed. Instead, there had been visits to a 'ladies' specialist'—her mother coming home late, looking worried but forcing a bright smile. Helen's imagination had run riot in the realms of the unknown, but she had obediently followed her mother's lead, pretending nothing was wrong. The news of the operation, and of the weeks of rest that Mum would need after it, had been a bombshell. Of the actual nature of the operation Mum had said little, obviously embarrassed— "it's ladies' trouble, darling, you know"—although how Helen was to know, if she herself did not tell her, was not clear.

At the sight of Jess's face, alarmingly grim, a new and terrible idea occurred to her.

"She hasn't got *cancer*..."

"NO! I never heard ... no, sorry, not your fault. Look, you can put that right out of your mind. 'Ladies' trouble', indeed ... Helen, have you ever heard of a hysterectomy?"

Helen had not, but after listening to the clear, concise explanation which Jess proceeded to give her, she almost felt that she could have done one herself. Why hadn't Mum told her any of this?

"Got that straight now? Good." Jess gazed at her thoughtfully. "I suppose Barbara has at least explained the facts of life to you?"

Her mother had tried to do something of the sort several times, using baby words and turning a painful red. Helen, who had picked up a working knowledge at school, had interrupted on the last occasion, to save her mother further agony—"Don't worry, Mum, I know all about that"—because it was all so very awkward, and Mum, obviously relieved, had stopped. There were still many things about which she was far from certain, but she didn't yet know Jess well enough to risk what would almost certainly prove to be a cripplingly embarrassing talk. So she answered quickly, as she had her mother:

"Of course I know all about that." Jess looked doubtful, but did not pursue it; Helen had the feeling that she knew it was a lie, and thought less of her for it.

Chapter Four

⟶ ❉ ❉ ⟵

THE SKIES HAD burst open during the night, and Tuesday was dull, wet and grey—brooding dark clouds, misted windows, huge puddles on West Haysham's uneven roads and pavements, and a steady drizzle.

It was typical first-day-back weather. Soaking children stamped muddily in the cloakrooms and steamed against the hot-water pipes. Coats dripped; the cloakroom floors were awash. Mrs. Page bustled around unperturbed, stripping off wet garments, restoring order from chaos.

Helen's five year-mates were already sitting round their table, talking hard.

"Helen will fit in nicely," said Mrs. Page. "Five of you round a six-place table, very convenient. Yes, Janice, I'm coming, I heard you the first time. *And* the second." She made the introductions and hurried off.

Helen slid into the vacant seat. The group were placed two on either side and one at each end of the oblong table; she found herself on a long side, facing the wall, with the boy, Paul Blakely, all freckles and dark spiky hair, on her right. Opposite stared the familiar, pasty face of Beverley Simmons.

"We thought you'd like to sit by Paul," said Joanne

Barclay. "We hear you like boys. We know you went to tea at the Pargeters'." She gazed, unblinking, at Helen, who was unsure if 'we' meant the whole table, or if Joanne chose to use the royal plural.

"Aren't we *kind* to you, Paul? Well, you know, to sit by a girl who *likes boys*." Paul, lean body hunched, growled inaudibly and shifted a few inches to his right. Helen, stiffening, moved imperceptibly to the left.

"We hope you won't find it too much of a comedown, being here," Joanne said. "We're probably rather different to what you're used to."

"Different *from*," Helen said automatically. There was a startled silence.

"Well, listen to that!" Joanne said at last. "We'll have to remember to talk properly, girls, won't we? Different *from*," she trilled in imitation. "You must excuse me if I forget and drop an 'h' now and then." Helen was silent. She could have bitten her tongue out. "I was very badly brought up, wasn't I, Lorraine? I expect *you'd* like to come round and tell my Mum how badly she brought me up. Would you?" Joanne wrinkled her nose, turned away and began whispering with Lorraine, both of them giggling and casting occasional glances at Helen.

As first impressions go, it couldn't have been much worse. If she could only put the clock back five minutes it could all be so different . . . Flushing pink, she gazed at the wall, but could see nothing but Joanne's hostile, square, freckled face. Joanne was as sturdy as Paul was lean; she would have been a picture of health but for her right arm, which was encased in white plaster.

Paul emerged from his morose silence to enquire about this.

"Joanne fell off Star," Lorraine said proudly, as if this was a particularly clever thing to do, only possible for someone of Joanne's calibre. "If she hadn't been thrown clear she could very easily have been killed."

"Three places," said Joanne, who had apparently appointed Lorraine spokesman on the topic of her accident.

"It broke in three places," said Lorraine, neatly picking up her cue. "They said in the hospital it was one of the nastiest fractures they'd seen in a long time."

"You won't be able to write," Melanie observed. Joanne smirked, greatly enjoying her special status. Helen was becoming the focus of much interested attention, as word spread around the Juniors that a stranger was in their midst. Newcomers were a rarity in West Haysham. Her back began to itch. Opposite, Beverley Simmons gazed in accusation.

"I saw you go past, didn't I. Twice. Why didn't you stop?" Beverley seemed to possess a particular talent for asking unanswerable questions; Helen could hardly say the truth: "I didn't want to talk to you". She muttered something about having been in a hurry. Her voice had gone cracked, she noticed dismally. That was Joanne's fault.

"Quiet!" roared Mrs. Page. "Assembly." Thirty-three chairs scraped backwards, and the Juniors trooped into the Infants' room. Helen felt lost. Even the tiniest Infants all knew each other. They all belonged. They all knew the routine. She was an outsider. The rain, relentless, beat against the windows.

The morning unwound, with Joanne intermittently chanting "Different *from*" and reminding the others to mind their grammar. Helen wondered if it was like this for her mother, new girl in a hospital ward. She doubted it. At Break she dawdled to let Joanne get well ahead; Richard Pargeter said 'Hi', nodding at her, but nothing more. She waited for the last person, Beverley, to go, intending to follow at a distance, but Beverley waited.

"Come on, you can't stay indoors, you know, it's stopped raining. You can walk around with me, if you like."

Helen was far from sure that she did like, but, outside, it occurred to her that at least she was less conspicuous than she would have been alone. Beverley plodded around the edge of the playground, giving a lengthy account of her sister's wedding, at which Beverley had been a bulging bridesmaid. Helen made interested noises at intervals.

"The bell should have gone by the time we get back," Beverley said. "Break is boring, isn't it? You don't talk much, do you? Anyway, there were two hundred people at the reception . . ."

Indoors, Lorraine was organizing a queue to sign Joanne's plaster cast. "She broke it in three places . . . could very easily have been killed," she was saying, while Joanne nodded bravely.

"Enough," Mrs. Page said, seeing this and coming over. "Break finished three minutes ago. Well, young lady, you're going to have problems this term, aren't you? Have you tried writing with your other hand? No, somehow I thought not . . ."

"Stupid woman," said Paul with disdain, finishing the ARSENAL F.C. he was scribbling on the plaster. For a startling moment he seemed to be talking about Mrs. Page. "Falling off a horse. Just like a stupid woman."

"Never mind, next term you'll be at the Chase," Mrs. Page said cheerfully. "You'll find things rather more balanced there."

"Yeah, and I'll have to give up my paper round, won't I." Paul shook his head gloomily. There was no justice. "My brother's taking it over. Keep it in the family."

"That's Paul's brother, over there," Melanie told Helen, pointing to a miniature replica of Paul on the third group table.

"He's not very different to Paul," Helen said, hoping to make amends for her earlier disaster, but nobody noticed. Joanne was getting bored with talk of paper rounds.

"I just thought," she said, "we'll have to be extra specially careful of what we say now. *Helen* will be telling Miss Cottis all about it."

Helen was stung. "I am *not* going to spy for Aunt Jess."

A voice said sharply: "Helen, while you're in school it's Miss Cottis. Right? I hardly thought I'd need to tell you." Joanne gurgled with delight; Helen bit her lip and mumbled an apology. Mrs. Page and her big ears. Joanne Barclay was probably Mrs. Page's favourite person.

At ten to twelve Helen was summoned to the telephone.

"My darling! How are you? How is school?" Mum! It was a relief to hear the familiar voice, but the conversation was not a success. Helen was unwilling to talk about school, which was fairly disastrous, so far; her mother was equally reluctant to discuss the hospital, and persisted with enquiries about 'your first day'. After some minutes of dodging and parrying, Helen wished her mother all the best for tomorrow, which hardly seemed adequate, under the circumstances, and, yes, she'd be talking to her again soon, and that was that. Somewhat flattened, she trailed out of the office, back to Joanne and purgatory. Mum never told her anything.

Mrs. Pargeter turned up for the afternoon. She had been organizing. She had a plan. The Juniors, she announced, were to hold a table tennis championship—a mini-Wimbledon all of their own.

"Wimbledon starts the day we come back from half-term," she explained, "so we'll get our tournament out of

33

the way first. We don't want to overshadow Messrs. Borg and McEnroe too much. I've made a list of seeds and an umpires' rota—we'll have the whole school in to watch the final. I'm sorry, you'll be out of it, Joanne, but I've made you Chief Umpire by way of consolation. I didn't know if you could play, Helen . . . you can, good . . . so I'm afraid you're unseeded." Helen was in fact a very good player for her age; they'd played a lot at Craddock House. She might be in with a chance, here.

"We'll get no work done today, I can see," said Mrs. Page, Mrs. Pargeter having departed to rummage in the store cupboard. "You can take your pick, a quiz or a story."

"Story!" shouted the Juniors, unanimously choosing the option which involved less mental exertion. The story, read briskly and uninspiringly by Mrs. Page, and interrupted by floor-shaking bangs from the store cupboard, was, in Helen's opinion, both corny and babyish; she was thoroughly bored by it.

Beverley Simmons was waiting in the cloakroom after school.

"You can walk home with me, if you like. You live nearly opposite, don't you?" Beverley had a peculiar way of talking; she turned nearly everything into a question, or ended it with 'if you like'. Both had the unnerving effect of throwing the responsibility for her every remark on to the other person. "Did I tell you about my bridesmaid dress? It was pale, pale blue . . ."

"To match your pale, pale face," thought Helen, searching for a way to divert this apparently endless matrimonial flow. Suddenly she caught sight of a face she knew.

"Alex! Hello. Did you get your hair for breakfast?" Alex Pargeter, lost in his duffle coat, turned a blank face to her, the whole porridge/hair business obviously long-forgotten. Mark, by his side, began to snigger, and somebody said: "Hare for breakfast? The new girl eats hare for breakfast!" Helen hated being called 'the new girl'; feeling an absolute fool, she hurried away from the gathering crowd. Beverley had observed all this with interest, but said no more than: "You are funny, aren't you?"

It wasn't until she reached the front door that it occurred to Helen that there was only one set of keys; Jess had that, and she couldn't get in. It had not been a good day.

"What's this about you eating hares at breakfast?" Joanne began the next day, before Helen had even sat down. Joanne always seemed to know about everything. Perhaps Helen was being bugged. The Essex Watergate. "I suppose you eat rabbits too. Rabbits aren't much different *from* hares. I suppose you eat them raw. That's disgusting. You've no right to go frightening my brother, talking about eating raw rabbits."

"*What* brother?"

"Mark, of course. How many brothers do you think I've got?"

Mark. The silent spy. The little snake. The informant in the midst of the Pargeters. How was she to guess that the little rat was Joanne's brother?

"And another thing. You stop picking on the Infants, right? I don't know who you think you are, coming here and upsetting little children. You leave poor little Alex alone. He hates you. He thinks you're a lunatic."

Helen knew no way of countering this. It was all completely beyond her experience—she had no training for such a battle. It seemed to be sheer, unprovoked, meaningless spite, and she couldn't compete. Unable to retaliate, she withdrew into silence. But in her mind she formed a counter-insult to every barb of Joanne's, and flashed at

35

her mentally what she dared not say aloud. This, after a while, became something of a comfort.

If Helen was preoccupied, Beverley was blandly oblivious of the fact. Whenever Helen left the room, there was Beverley, stolid, expressionless, patiently waiting for her. In a way it was rather flattering; Beverley was not unlike a large dog—undemanding, not too hot at witty conversation, but always there at your side. Not that she ever showed even a glimmer of friendship inside the classroom, where it was most needed. She was probably far too scared of Joanne, Helen thought. Joanne could demolish Beverley in seconds, without even trying. Helen would have preferred a dog. At least they were loyal.

"You can come round on Saturday, if you like," Beverley said indifferently after lunch. "Come round the back of the pub." Helen had visions of albums of wedding photographs. She wasn't sure that she had enough interested noises left to cope with that. Still, you could never tell; on her home ground Beverley might undergo a transformation, like Cinderella or, considering Beverley's shape, like the pumpkin turning into the coach—and become a vivacious, entertaining hostess. Just like pigs might fly. "As much free Coke and crisps as we like..." Beverley was saying. This sounded very satisfactory.

Jess was beckoning urgently from the door of the Infants' room.

"I just rang the hospital," she said in a low voice. "The op. went perfectly—your mother's just coming round. Nothing to worry about at all. O.K.?"

"O.K.," Helen said, beaming, her nagging fear of the surgeon's scalpel dismissed for ever. She was still smiling as she took her seat.

"Here comes the rabbit," said Joanne. "Bugs Bunny's back in town."

You are beneath contempt, Helen told her silently. You are lower than an ant. Lower than a baked bean.

"We know *all* about you. You came from a *snob* school. Where you didn't have to mix with *common* people like us. Didn't you?"

You are lower than a *common* baked bean.

"Give it a rest, woman," snarled Paul. "You're worse than our Mum."

At the end of school Mrs. Page asked Helen to stay behind, and ushered her through to the Infants' room, where Jess was sitting talking to Mrs. Pargeter, with a tall bottle on the table.

"Ah, here she is," Mrs. Pargeter said cheerfully. Jess smiled and picked up the bottle.

"We thought we'd have a quick celebratory drink, Helen. To Barbara's speedy recovery. I popped home and fetched a bottle of five-year-old sherry—definitely celebration quality." She poured a small glass for her niece. "Mrs. Pargeter's boys often drink wine, French habit, very civilized. No, *sip* it!" Helen had taken an ordinary mouthful and was now choking violently. "Oh, Lord. Have you never tasted sherry before?" Helen had not, and sincerely hoped she never would again. Recovering, though she was sure she could still feel sherry swishing about in her nose, she sipped the tawny gold drink very gingerly. It was quite horrible, but it wouldn't do to admit this. Helen didn't want a reputation for not being able to hold her alcohol, especially if the Pargeters were such seasoned drinkers.

The teachers were obviously so happy for her that she felt guilty for not being able to share their pleasure a hundred per cent. Now, if Joanne Barclay were to fall down a manhole, she'd drink the entire bottle, and ask for more.

She walked home at Jess's side, wondering miserably if Joanne would ever leave her alone. She might never stop—this might go on all term. Helen didn't think she could bear that. She thought that the best thing might be to ask her aunt for help. Surely Jess would do something to stop it. But that evening, while they were setting out the backgammon pieces, Jess said:

"This is all very hard for Joanne, you know. She's such an active girl as a rule, always riding. The sedentary life must be slow torture for her, she's never been much of a reader. She's bored to death."

And that was that. It was impossible to expect anything of Jess now; she might just as well have said: "Don't come whining to *me* for help. Joanne Barclay isn't only Mrs. Page's favourite person, she's mine, as well."

Chapter Five

❧ ✾ ✾ ❧

BY THE END OF that first week Helen was settling into the routine of West Haysham School. Mornings were spent round the tables, in the groups, all working at their different levels; afternoons were much more flexible, and often given over to games, painting, singing or team quizzes. On the surface the atmosphere in the classroom was casual and relaxed, but the Juniors were careful not to go too far—nobody wanted to risk a lash of Mrs. Page's tongue.

This was sharper than the flick of a whip, and a good deal louder. Mrs. Page had a terrible temper, which boiled up in an instant and died away just as quickly, as if someone had turned the gas off underneath her. The temper had a different trigger-point every day; what was unthinkable cheek on one day might be quite amusing on another. Cheek was the worst crime of all. It was like living on the edge of a volcano, much given to short, sharp, unpredictable eruptions. The West Haysham children knew their volcano of old, and were quick to get out of the way when it started to make dangerous noises, but Helen found it alarming and confusing, and grew very wary of Mrs. Page.

The work itself was no trouble, far easier than at Craddock House. Helen rapidly began to acquire rows of red ticks and a number of gold stars. Joanne, unable to write, sitting in boredom with a list of words to learn for spelling, eyed her with scorn.

"So the rabbit's a little swot, is it. Bunny Brain of Britain. It must be the lettuce that does it. Or perhaps they teach you better at snob schools."

You have the brain of a retarded peanut, said Helen from behind her walls of silence.

Friday was a library afternoon. Joanne and Lorraine presided officiously with box of tickets and date stamp. Helen returned *Heidi* and decided to try *Watership Down*, which she'd heard a good deal about from various people. She presented the book open, ready to be stamped; Joanne flipped it shut with interest.

"Look!" she squealed with relish. "The rabbit wants to read about its relatives!" Lorraine collapsed in a heap, holding her sides. Giggles from all around. Helen snatched the book back—it was now spoiled for ever—and slammed it back on the shelf. She did not use the school library again.

The weekend was a blessed relief. Helen arrived at the back of the Fountain on Saturday afternoon to find Beverley curled up on a chair, reading a teenage magazine. She stared up at Helen reproachfully, as if she had forgotten inviting her.

"I'm not too early, am I?"

Beverly reluctantly lowered the magazine. "I suppose not. I've just done this quiz, look. It's to test your sense of humour. I scored 24. That means I've got a tremendous sense of fun and I'm always the centre of attention at parties. D'you want a go?" Helen doubted the accuracy of this, but obediently answered the questions. She scored eleven.

"'You tend to be a wet blanket at times,'" read Beverley, pleased. "'Try not to take yourself so seriously.' Never mind. We can't all be the centre of attention, can we? They're very good, these quizzes. I always get the best score. I've discovered a lot about myself. D'you want a Coke?"

Helen followed her hostess through to the public bar, empty at this time of day. Mr. Simmons, stomach bulging and rounded, was propped against the bar, studying a list of figures.

"Hello, my angel. Is this your new little friend?" Helen winced. "Now, who are we today? Helen, is it? Our Bev's got that many different friends I can't keep track of the names. Someone new every week."

Did Beverley have a troupe of unknown friends, visiting on a rotation system, like Helen's breakfast cereals? Or did nobody, having once visited, ever come back?

"Can we have Coke and crisps, Dad?"

Mr. Simmons smiled fondly at his daughter. "You could do a lot worse than have our Bev for a friend, little lady. She's a smasher, if I do say so myself. All we've got left now our Wendy's married." Beverley appeared unmoved by this awful talk. "I dare say Bev'll tell you about the wedding, if you ask her. You could show ... er ... Helen your bridesmaid dress, love."

"These are plain, Dad. Haven't you got Salt and Vinegar?" Mr. Simmons rummaged for another box.

"That's right." Beverley seized two bags and the opened bottles and departed; Helen, feeling for the unnoticed parent, took two chunky pub glasses and followed.

"You'd think he'd know by now that I prefer Salt and Vinegar. Fathers are awful, aren't they?"

"I wouldn't know. I haven't got one."

"Haven't you? You are funny. Oh well. What's on the

41

telly?" She switched the set on, cramming crisps into her mouth. Helen settled back to watch the athletics. It was as good a way to pass the afternoon as any. A high-jumper was poised to run. "Patterson's third and last try at this height," said Ron Pickering. Patterson drew himself up, began to run.

"Stupid sport, all there ever is on Saturday afternoons." Beverley switched off, cutting Patterson off in mid-stride. Suddenly it seemed very important to know if Patterson would have cleared the bar. "I hate that, athletics," Beverley said through a mouthful of crisps. "I hate all games, don't you? Mrs. Pargeter's always on at me, nag, nag, nag. I hate Mrs. Pargeter."

Helen wondered how long she was expected to stay. At least nothing had been said about tea. This was a rotten afternoon. *Logan* was better company than Beverley. Perhaps she might start to make leaving noises in about half an hour.

"I do think Joanne Barclay is a bitch, don't you?" Beverley said, breaking into her thoughts. This was undeniable, but Helen had learned by now to be careful. She would not have been surprised to find Brother Mark in the cupboard, taking notes. So she paraphrased Jess's earlier remarks:

"She is a bit, at the moment, but I expect she's bored. It must be awful for a horsy sort of girl to have to sit around all day."

This answer did not please Beverley, who sniffed. There followed a long silence, Helen racking her brains for something to break it.

"Who was that girl I saw you with last Sunday in the garden?" she asked after a while.

"That's Michelle. She's fourteen, she goes to the Chase." Beverley spoke as if Helen should have known this. "She's got a boyfriend, Steve. He's dishy. He fancies me. But you don't pinch your friend's boyfriend," she added virtuously. "Anyway, I've got one of my own."

This was too much. Something inside Helen snapped.

"Don't be so soft. You're too young to have boyfriends."

Beverley bridled. "Are you calling me a liar?"

"Yes."

"Well, I like that! I let you be my friend and ask you round and give you free Coke and crisps and who do you think *you* are to say if I've got a boyfriend or not? If that's how you're going to be you'd better go home."

"I think I'll do that," Helen said, getting up, and joining the ranks of friends who visited and left, never to return, before Mr. Simmons had time to learn their names.

She should have seen straight away that something was very wrong. Joanne Barclay was listening intently to Beverley; normally she took no more notice of her than she would of a fly. Melanie Davies turned huge brown eyes to Helen, looking distressed; Paul, ignoring them, drew a ferocious dinosaur on the back of an exercise book.

"Well, here it comes," Beverley said nastily. "'Joanne Barclay is a proper bitch,' she said. And then that you couldn't stand having your arm in plaster 'cos you're too thick to read a book."

Oh, you poisonous fat slug.

Beverley was relishing the rare treat of being the centre of attention.

"She took crisps and Coke from our bar without even saying thank you. I like that, don't you? And then she started on at me. She said she doesn't believe I've got a boyfriend."

"Of course you haven't," Helen said. Joanne leapt into attack.

"You leave my friend Beverley alone. Who *do* you think you are, coming from your snob school and upsetting people who've lived here all their lives?"

Your *friend*? O.K., Joanne Barclay. You're welcome to her. You deserve each other. Next Saturday *you* can go and spend the afternoon in her rotten pub.

"Too much talking over here." Mrs. Page approached the table. "If I can't trust my oldest group ... and wipe that insolent look off your face, Joanne. Have you learned that spelling list? Right, over to my desk and I'll test you."

You fool, Helen Keates. You trusting little fool. Everyone in this entire lousy manure-ridden village hates you ... Gritting her teeth, she vowed that from now on she would talk to *nobody*. It would only get twisted round and reported back to Joanne. She should have been in the Gestapo. Hitler would have loved her. He'd have given her a concentration camp all of her own.

"How do you spell 'occasionally'?" Melanie was whispering. Helen gazed at her icily, her face a mask. Here was another one, coming over all sweetness and light the moment Joanne turned her back. Not again, thank you. Melanie shrugged and found a dictionary.

Helen took a piece of scrap paper and calculated how much of the term was left. 301 hours. They'd been here nearly an hour today, so call it three hundred. She would get through that, somehow, and then she'd never have to see anyone in this *bloody* village again. Bloody, like damn and hell, was forbidden by her mother—although she had heard Mum, when fraught, use all three in the same breath—but she was beyond caring.

Gradually, Helen began to function more like a machine than a human being, reacting to nothing, answering only mechanically when Mrs. Page spoke to her. She got through the days by sticking to a strict routine, clinging to it as to a lifeboat. Without this she would have sunk. Nothing that Joanne said or did could make any day better or worse than all the rest. They were all the same—seven hours, to be survived and crossed off the slowly diminishing total.

The mornings were the worst. After Jess called her Helen wallowed for a moment in peaceful half-dreams, then, with a sickening *glunk* she woke, and remembered. It was like going to the dentist every single day. She only got herself out of bed at all by telling herself: "Just get through today and that's seven hours less to go."

Robotlike she dressed, breakfasted on the cereal of the day and walked to school with Jess. Until the bell rang she hid in the lavatories, listening to the drip, drip, of the cold tap on the end basin and the gurgling of the pipes. She became very familiar with the school plumbing. Then work. Thanks to her fierce concentration, Helen's marks stayed as high as ever. The one who suffered, markwise, was in fact Joanne. Bored, irritated by Helen's total lack of response, Joanne could do nothing right, and was regularly blasted by Mrs. Page.

"*Don't* think you can idle the term away because of a broken arm. You're going to the Chase next term and if you carry on like this I doubt if they'll have a stream low enough for you. They'll have to have five streams, A, B, C, D and Joanne Barclay. You'll be a disgrace to West Haysham..." Joanne, pink and angry, blamed Helen.

The afternoons were generally better. Since Beverley's defection Helen had been spending lunchtime in solitude, leaning against the wall, her back to the school and the noise of the school game being played. Immobile, she stared out over the golf course. She was never disturbed;

45

Joanne had no wish to waste precious free time on rabbit-baiting. Once the afternoon started, it was often possible to get away from the top group table, and if Mrs. Page noticed anything odd in Helen's behaviour, she gave no sign of it.

By the end of the third week Helen had amassed a veritable constellation of stars and her team, the Bears, had shot to the top with a clear lead. (The Muppet-mad Juniors had pleaded for, and been granted, teams called Bears, Frogs, Gophers and Swedish Chefs.) After the Bears' third consecutive win, Mrs. Page deliberated for a while, and came to the conclusion that Helen would have to be transferred to the Gophers, to balance the deficit which was being caused mainly by Joanne Barclay.

"*Charming*, isn't it, Joanne?" Beverley said haughtily. Joanne grunted. The charms of Beverley Simmons had rapidly palled; it had never been a friendship, just an anti-Helen alliance.

After school Helen hung around, picking up bits of paper from the floor so assiduously that Mrs. Page made her Tidiness Monitor. She felt this quite undeserved, since she only did it to give Joanne a good head start. Fortunately Joanne was not one to spend one second longer than necessary in school. Helen ran home at top speed, always expecting Joanne to be lurking behind a bush or to drop on her from a tree, let herself in with the spare key Jess had had cut, and slammed the door. Safe.

It was good to be alone—she savoured the silence of the house, sitting still, unwilling to break it. She almost resented the arrival of Jess—always cheerful, but reminding her of school.

It was no good. Aunt Jess was no longer just Aunt Jess, she was Miss Cottis as well. And while Aunt Jess might not be expected to understand what her niece was going through, Miss Cottis should know. Miss Cottis should do something. But Miss Cottis just said:

"Mrs. Page says you're very quiet, Helen. She's known parrots chattier than you. Try and join in a bit more. Aren't you getting to know the others, now?"

Helen wondered how best to dodge this one. It seemed safest to misunderstand the question.

"I know everyone's *first* name. That's easy. When Mrs. Page says a name you just look to see who answers. I don't know your form. Well, the Pargeters, and Sherrilyn Comfort." This name had seemed so unbelievable that Helen had taken the trouble to identify its owner, a disappointingly dull child, all buck teeth.

Helen filled her letters to her mother with harmless details like Sherrilyn. The letters had to be carefully worded; Mum, now safely with Alison, was a recuperating invalid, and must not be worried. Letters arrived from Devon every week, more post than Helen had received before in her life—letters that said how much Mum was missing Helen, that begged for more information about school, that sent Alison's love—that was a good joke—and were loaded with terrible things like:

"I shan't be really better till I've got my darling back with me..." Helen imagined Joanne reading that, and blanched.

In return she wrote about her health, Jess's health, her school marks and the dreadful weather. It was perhaps just as well that Jess wasn't on the phone. Helen was rapidly learning the art of writing a good deal without actually saying anything at all. Saying nothing was starting to be second nature.

Chapter Six

➤ ❋ ❋ ⇐

"YOU CERTAINLY DON'T bring good weather with you," Jess said as they walked to school, huddled under her umbrella. "We'll be having a swimming gala in the playground if this keeps up."

The papers were saying that it was the wettest start to May for over half a century. Helen could well believe it. Nobody bothered to comment on the rain any more—it was taken for granted. There was flooding in parts of East Anglia, and all attempts to get the cricket season under way were being wetly foiled.

There was little opportunity for games in West Haysham, either. As rainy afternoon followed rainy afternoon, Mrs. Page and Mrs. Pargeter put their heads together and decided that the Table Tennis Championships might as well get started.

"Thirty-two exactly, with Joanne injured," said Mrs. Pargeter approvingly. Even numbers dared not disobey Mrs. Pargeter. "Four rounds and then the final." She produced a large chart, neatly marked out with black lines ready for names to be filled in as the draw was made, and the one space—'Winner'—at which sixty-four eyes now looked with longing.

"Do it like the F.A. Cup," said Paul Blakely. "Two people taking turns to pull out balls with numbers on. We ought to get Ted Croker down to call the names out."

"Certainly, Paul, if you can produce thirty-two numbered balls." Paul meditated, loath to give up his scheme.

"Numbers on bits of paper, folded up. Just go down the register, number people from one to thirty-two."

"That's what I like, initiative," said Mrs. Pargeter. "Who shall we have to draw the numbers?"

Mrs. Page suggested the oldest and youngest in the school. "Staff excluded," she added hastily. "Come on up here, Melanie, and Helen, would you pop next door and ask Miss Cottis if we can borrow her youngest? Explain what we want it for, and that it will be returned intact in a quarter of an hour or so."

Helen slipped through the door and stopped, surprised. Her aunt was barely visible, seated in the middle of a pack of squirming Infants. One tiny girl was clutching Jess's skirt, and gazing ferociously at everyone else. The babble of high-pitched Infant voices died down as they became aware of the presence of an intruder, and the crowd moved even closer to Jess, as if Helen might have come to take her from them.

"What can I . . . Lisa, my skirt, *please*! . . . do for you, Helen?"

Helen, fascinated, ignored the wrathful glare of Lisa and explained her errand.

"Nicky Bailey," said Jess, extracting a small blond boy from the adoring throng. "Now, stand *back*, all of you . . . *skirt*, Lisa . . ."

"Why did you decide to be a teacher, Aunt Jess?" Helen asked casually that night. She was stacking the backgammon pieces, black and white alternately, into a tower.

49

Logan, disgruntled by the ceaseless drizzle, watched, wondering at the ridiculous things humans did when they could be out catching mice, or pursuing the Latchfords' comely young tabby.

"It was just what I wanted to do. And, I suppose, because I knew I'd be good at it. I'd had plenty of practice with Barbara, so I knew something of the machinations of the infant mind."

Logan stretched out a paw and sent Helen's tower crashing down.

"My Gran—your mother—how old were you when she died?"

"Nineteen. She was old having me, positively geriatric when Barbara came along, and Dad was older still. He couldn't really have brought up a ten-year-old on his own. So there was only me. So I did it."

Her mother had never said anything about this.

"You looked after Mum on your own? While you were teaching?"

"I wasn't teaching then. I went straight out to work. Worked in a bank in Stambury till Barbara left school. Hated every minute of it. To this day I shudder when I have to cross the threshold of Barclays. So I quit and trained as a teacher. Best thing I ever did. There you are, the Life of Jessica Cottis, Abridged Version. When *Who's Who* write asking for details I shall refer them to you. Now, let's have some music." She had been sorting idly through a box of cassettes. "See what you think of this. *War of the Worlds*. Christmas present."

"But it's a *talking* thing." Helen said after a moment.

"Quiet. Listen."

Helen pulled her writing-pad over, meaning to write a long-overdue letter to Deborah, but five minutes later she had put her pen down, needing all her attention for the music. When Jess finally clicked the machine shut, well over an hour later, Helen still had not moved. She was transfixed.

"I gather you liked it."

Helen could not think of words that came near to describing how much she had liked it. "Can we have it on again? Now?"

"Good Lord, no. It's far too long to play twice in one night. Ask me later in the week." Jess looked at her more closely. "You are the most peculiar girl, Helen. That's the first time I've seen a trace of animation in your face for a fortnight. If you aren't careful you might actually smile."

"Not a lot to smile about."

"Oh, *Helen*. Don't be so hopeless. Your mother's making a marvellous recovery, you're doing extremely well at school—yes you are, I'll tell you, in confidence, and I mean in confidence, Mrs. Page is very impressed with your work. She thinks you could have a brilliant career. And to look at you anyone would think you were a starving orphan. You can't expect everything to be perfect."

How beastly of Jess to turn a beautiful evening into a lecture, Helen thought angrily, coming back down to earth with a bump. How could Jess know what it was like to wake up every single morning dreading the day ahead . . . She had forgotten about Jess's eight years in the bank.

War of the Worlds was likely to be in the village library. She'd go along after school and see. Withdrawing from the school library had left Helen bookless; this was intolerable, and she was forced to ask Jess about the local library, which proved to be rather smaller than the Infants' formroom. The contents of the children's shelves strongly reflected local interest. Helen gazed with distaste at *Suzy's First Pony*. There was probably an entire series, working through *Suzy's Second Pony* to her tenth, then graduating to *Suzy's First Horse*, ending with *Suzy Buys a Racecourse*. In West Haysham, horses and ponies seemed to have a fatal fascination for anyone female and under fourteen; hence all the horsy books. Perhaps *War of the Worlds* would be there too, sandwiched between a couple of geldings.

Of course, she had to get through her first round match in the Tournament first. Everyone had enjoyed the draw—it was smashing, being drawn out of a bag just like Liverpool or Chelsea—and Helen had been more than satisfied with her first opponent. Fiona Baldwin was a skinny, giggly ten-year-old who held a table tennis bat gingerly with the ends of her fingers, as if afraid that it might leap up of its own accord and beat her about the head. She'd murder Fiona Baldwin.

She nearly did, too. A fair crowd gathered round the table to watch the first performance of the unknown quantity. By the time they had all settled the unknown quantity was leading fourteen-love. Fiona giggled weakly, occasionally managing to hit a ball back over the net. Helen took pity on her and sent a couple of backhands wide, finally winning 21–2.

Mrs. Pargeter was impressed. "I'd have seeded you if I'd known you could play like that." Helen could in fact play a good deal better than that, given a decent opponent, but she had no intention of letting this be known yet. She caught the eye of Joanne Barclay, who did not look pleased.

Two of the seeds were playing today, Paul and Lorraine. Helen paid close attention to their matches. She thought she could cope with Lorraine, who was very weak on the backhand. Paul would be a lot harder; she almost panicked, seeing his fast returns and sharp reactions, and a spin-serve which was still in the experimental stage. She pulled herself together, concentrated. Find his weak points.

Paul was showing off now, knowing himself to be the best player in the school, hot favourite for the title. She glanced at the chart. Paul was in the other half of the draw. If she could beat Lorraine, and she was pretty sure of that, she'd meet him in the final. Her eyes slid back to the match, saw Paul try a fancy return which missed the table by a foot. He was leading 18–2 now, and had started to fool around, confident of an easy win.

That might be the only way to beat him. She would have to let him get ahead, start relaxing and lose concentration. *Then* she'd start to play.

Not that she particularly disliked Paul Blakely. At times she was very grateful for his habit of telling Joanne to shut up. Joanne wasn't above teasing him, but warily; she took notice of Paul. Over the years the top group had evolved a sort of hierarchy. Beverley was the lowest of the low; Paul, however outnumbered, was on top, just by an edge. Helen understood all this well.

Herself still a total stranger to the other five, she felt by now that *she* knew *them*. Beverley was just a lump. Melanie Davies, unusual with her jet black hair and skin so pale it was almost white, was liked by everyone; quiet, a hard worker, though not especially clever, often seeming years older than the others. A couple of times she had said softly to Helen: "Don't take any notice, they don't mean it," but Helen wanted no more 'friends' after Beverley, and had pretended not to hear.

Skinny, lank-haired Lorraine Roberts, who apparently asked no more of life than to breathe the same air as did Joanne, turned out to be something of a dark horse; she had the brains for both of them, and generally did the work for both of them, too. On the few occasions when Helen had seen her alone, out of school, Lorraine had nodded in an everyday, nice-to-see-you way. It was bewildering. Lorraine, as distinct from Joanne-and-Lorraine, seemed to have nothing against her at all.

All the hate came from Joanne. It flowed from her like dark poison, fuelling Beverley, sparking off Lorraine. Helen no longer wondered why. The truth might be so awful that it was better not to know. Perhaps she really did smell bad. Perhaps she did all sorts of disgusting things that everyone at Craddock House had been too polite to mention. She felt almost as if she should find a bell and walk round like a leper, chanting: "Unclean, unclean, unclean."

Chapter Seven

$\Rightarrow * * \Leftarrow$

"No, I'm sorry, you can't have this," the librarian said, taking *War of the Worlds* from Helen's hand and placing it firmly out of reach. "Adults. You're not allowed adult books." It was ridiculous. There was the book, here was Helen, and this *stupid* librarian wouldn't let her have it. It was outrageous.

"Could I just have it to look at, then? I'll be very careful . . ."

The librarian, startlingly elegant in an off-white suit which looked as if it might have originated in Paris, sighed patiently. "It's no good, dear. I don't make the rules. It's Adults. You're not. It might not be *suitable*." This made the book seem more desirable than ever. "Look, as you're looking so disappointed, I'll let you have something special. Brand new, not even on the shelves yet. *Gymkhana Julie*, by the author of *Suzy's First Pony*. There'll be a *queue* for this as soon as I put it out."

"Thank you, I don't like horse books," Helen said, feeling let down after the big build-up. She could see she was getting nowhere; it was like flogging a dead horse. It could only be a matter of time before somebody wrote *Suzy Flogs a Dead Horse*, and that would be a sure-fire hit down here, too.

She had thought the Children's Library empty, but when she rounded the partition, there was Richard Pargeter, sprawled awkwardly on a stool.

"Hi."

"Hi," Helen replied after a momentary hesitation. She felt a strong urge to go and check for a bugging device, or Mark Barclay, it amounted to the same thing.

"These stools are so stupid," Richard was saying in hushed, library tones. The stools were barely nine inches high, and would not comfortably accommodate anything larger than a four-year-old bottom.

"If they tried to put proper chairs in here there wouldn't be room for the books," Helen said, finding this conversation strange and difficult after her weeks of self-imposed isolation. It was surprising how quickly not-talking became a habit; her first instinct, on seeing Richard, had been to turn away sharply. Whatever it was about her that was so revolting must be quite as obvious to him as it was to Joanne. Richard, however, was treating her for all the world as if she were a normal human being. He had a book in his hand—*More Famous Sea Stories*. No doubt by the author of *Famous Sea Stories, Peter's First Raft* and *Paul Crosses the Atlantic Single-Handed in a Bathtub*.

Richard followed her eyes. "I like these." Helen remembered the *Cutty Sark*. "I'm going to join the Navy." Not 'I want to', but 'I'm going to'. She had no doubt that he would. How wonderful to have your future career all sorted out at twelve.

"I don't know what I'm going to do yet. I don't actually *want* to do anything in particular." Her voice sounded unnatural—she was out of practice when it came to small talk. Turning, she began to scan the shelves, but Richard seemed disposed to chat.

"It's good, that," he said, jabbing at a book on the floor. "I think I'll take it out. *Codes and Secret Languages*. Rita grapline dracker," he added surprisingly.

"Come again?" Richard looked gratified.

"That's me backwards. More or less. Richard Neil Pargeter. Andrew understands. Dad started us doing that. You've got to be careful, though. If you started shouting 'God!' at the dog they'd come in little white coats to put you away. Now I can't remember what I came here for. Oh yes I can. See if you can find a book that says how to make a kite. It's for Michael, a consolation prize. What he really wanted was a catapult."

"Why?"

"To keep Sherrilyn Comfort off. She's in love with him. He can't stand her."

"Wouldn't his bow and arrows do?"

"Not when she gets close. And it's when she gets close that the trouble starts. They're not proper arrows, anyway, they've got suckers on the end. But Dad reckoned if he had a catapult he'd likely kill her. She tries to hold his hand under the table."

Richard wrinkled his nose in disgust.

"Are you sure? Poor Michael."

"Poor Sherrilyn too, I suppose. She can't *help* being a moron and a softie. She goes round looking almost as miserable as you do."

Helen's yelp of indignation was luckily drowned by the noise of somebody coming into the library.

"I do *not* look like Sherrilyn Comfort."

"Of course you don't. You look worse. You go around staring at the ground, never a word to anybody. Here I've been talking to you for ten minutes and you've said about that many words. People think you're stuck up. I don't. I know why. It's Joanne Barclay."

Helen stiffened. "I don't talk about that."

"You don't talk about *anything*. You want to stand up to her, not just soak it up like a sponge."

"I do *not* want to. I'm not getting into arguments with Joanne Barclay. It'd be like David and Goliath."

"David won."

He was too clever by half, this one. "If I pretend not to hear, she stops. She gets bored if she thinks I don't care."

"Of course she knows you care, the way you wander round looking like a dead fish. Anyone could see there's something wrong."

"I wouldn't have thought they noticed me much."

"Don't be daft," he said, not unkindly. "You stick out like a sore thumb. Still, if you won't talk, people stop trying. Melanie's tried to make friends, she says you glare at her like she'd just murdered your mother. You can't go blaming the rest of the world for Joanne. You want to join in things sometimes."

Helen lowered herself cautiously on to a stool. This boy was very good at telling her what she wanted to do, she thought crossly.

"What difference would that make?"

"Show you don't care. Join in the game at lunchtime."

"But after so long . . . I *can't*."

"Of course you can. Look, if it's fine tomorrow I'll say I want you on my team, and you just join in. Joanne can't even play."

"Everyone would *look* at me, though."

"Won't kill you. Anyway, nobody's going to bother looking at you once the game starts. They'll be watching the ball."

What an extraordinary boy, calmly making all these arrangements without so much as consulting her. He reminded her of someone else, but she couldn't for the moment think who.

"I reckon you'll make a fair player," he told her, getting up to search for a kite-making book. "I watched your match today. You're good. You've got an eye for a ball. You'll beat me," he said, without resentment. "In the quarter-finals." Helen didn't deny it, knowing that, barring disaster, she would. Richard extracted a volume in triumph. "Yes, good. Chapter Four, Kite. Don't let Joanne upset you so much," he added offhandedly. "She's really not worth it."

Helen sniffed suddenly—the unexpected kindness was too much, and she could feel hot tears pricking the back of her eyes. She'd *die* if Richard Pargeter saw her cry... Hurrying out, she rubbed her eyes fiercely. It was idiotic; she'd sat through hours of torment without even a sniffle, and now, a few kind words from Richard Pargeter and she was howling like a baby.

The next morning was long remembered for the Explosion of the Term, if not the Explosion of the Year. The Juniors scored Mrs. Page's more violent eruptions in Goal of the Month fashion, Row X, Row Y, Row Z. It was quite an honour to have sparked off the worst row of the term. On this occasion the lucky one was Robin Blakely, though lucky was not a description he would have accepted at the time. What happened was that Robin, distracted by the unfamiliar sight of the sun shining outside, lost track of what Mrs. Page was saying. When she interrupted his trance to enquire sharply: "Robin, are you with me?" he absent-mindedly said: "No, I'm with the Woolwich," thus triggering off a roar which rocked the school.

After that, it was touch and go whether the Juniors would be kept in during the lunch hour, but Mrs. Page, forced to choose between retribution and her own peace and quiet, decided that retribution could wait.

Helen felt as if all eyes were on her, as they trooped out, salad and rhubarb crumble disposed of. She had half-hoped for rain but, having finally made an appearance, the sun seemed determined to stay. It was all very well for the Richard Pargeters of this world. But in the event it was something of an anticlimax; Richard grabbed her unceremoniously by the arm and pulled her into line behind him. There was a mild flutter of interest, but attention rapidly switched to the mounting argument about whose turn it was to be bowler.

"You know what to do?" Richard asked. Helen thought she did—she had listened often enough to the game being played. The West Haysham School game was something like a cross between rounders and cricket, adapted to suit the layout of the playground. Don't let me make a fool of myself, she prayed, picturing herself hitting the ball up for a catch, which would get the entire team out...

The queue was disappearing at an alarming rate. Now it was Richard's turn, cool as a cucumber in a freezer, whack and run, now Helen—Oh, God, please stop them all *looking* at me. At least the bowler was only Julie Chase. If it had been Paul Blakely... *Now*—Julie tossed the ball mildly at Helen—call that bowling?—there was a satisfactory thud, and a fielder spun round in pursuit of the ball. Helen was off in a flash, running her hardest.

"Home Run," called Joanne Barclay, perched on the dustbin which was the traditional umpire's seat. This was delightfully ironic; Joanne's status as umpire forced her to treat Helen as fairly as she did everyone else, or the entire team would turn on her. It was a pleasant change for Helen to have the numbers on her side. Lorraine, though a good player, was in dutiful attendance on Joanne. Their heads tilted together, and they conferred softly.

Helen, out of breath but triumphant, took her place back at the end of the queue. Richard gave her a nod of approval, and at once she knew who it was that he reminded her of. His mother. He's done *exactly* the same as she did, Helen realized, remembering the smooth way she had been dropped into the badminton game. A proper chip off the maternal block.

More table tennis matches were scheduled for the afternoon, and Helen chose to watch. She was sandwiched in, unable to move without disturbing the players, by the time she realized that Joanne and Lorraine were right behind her.

"So it's decided we're good enough to play games with now. We're so honoured. We ought to be licking its feet."

"*Ugh*. You'll make me ill."

"We mustn't call it rabbit now. What shall we call it, Lorraine?"

"Its Royal Highness."

"I know. We'll call it *Mole*."

Helen, who had a large mole on her neck, flushed and bit her lip.

"Its Royal *Mole*ness. *I* know why it came here," she went on, just loudly enough for Helen and the people surrounding her to catch every word. "Its mother was ill. You know why. All those years living with Mole drove her mad. She's insane. She's been put in a mental home."

Oh God, don't let me kill her. She's not worth going to prison for . . .

"That's the game, 21–14 to Rebecca," called Melanie, and in the general stirring that followed, Helen was able to slip away, giving no sign that inside she was longing to ram Joanne Barclay's head into a drainpipe.

Jess was suffering from a severe attack of cleaning-fever that evening. Helen found her, looking most un-Jesslike in an old pinafore, on hands and knees, vigorously scouring the oven.

"How about doing me a favour and nipping round to Hay House with a couple of bottles of carrot?" she asked, clearly wanting Helen out from under her feet. "I hear you got four Home Runs today," she added a moment later. "Very creditable. Is there *anything* you're not good at?"

Much flattered, Helen seized the two bottles, marked 'White Table Wine', and fled. She had no wish to be dragged into a spring-cleaning session.

Hay House was the home of the Wilkes sisters, opposite the Pargeters at Long Acre. Most West Haysham houses were known by name only; Helen liked this, and knew most of them already. The semi-detached house with all the gnomes in unlikely positions in the garden was Nirvana—Jess, when asked the meaning of this, had said something about Blissful Buddhists and the Seventh Heaven. Winalot was the place with the little black dog always snapping at the gate. Helen wasn't sure whether the owners had won the pools, or intended to have the house ground into biscuits and fed to the dog. Then there was a long, white-painted bungalow called Allegretto— she thought of this as a musical box. If the roof was lifted it might play a scherzo, very allegretto, through the windows. Jess would have nothing to do with this, insisting that Number 31 was all the name her house required.

"I went off house names when Doug and Sylvia French moved into a perfectly nice little cottage and called it Dougsyl. It's a wonder Biddy Morgan at the Pines hasn't changed it to Morbid."

Deborah would have had hysterics at that. One of the

worst things was no longer having anybody to share jokes with. However, the separation was not now so painful. At first, not a day had passed during which Helen had not thought back, at least once, to Craddock House, and worked out what her form would be doing at that moment. But by now Craddock House was neatly parcelled as a part of her life that was over. And, if she was honest, it was difficult to feel much nostalgia for the uncomfortable building, cramped classrooms, battered desks, strict regulations, horrible bottle-green uniform, ancient plumbing that always went wrong on the very coldest days. Before the move she had never known anything different, but now ... if only there was no Joanne Barclay. She could be having the time of her life this term, if there was no Joanne Barclay.

Helen banished Joanne from her thoughts. She was supposed to be delivering wine. The Wilkes sisters were local legends in their own lifetimes—Jess once said that invading Romans, wandering through this part of Essex, had come upon Hay House and the Wilkes sisters, decided it was as good a place as any, and had built the village of West Haysham around them.

At the time this had seemed wildly funny, but Helen could not help feeling slightly apprehensive as she walked along, wrinkling her nose at the manure smell which was particularly strong today. It was unlikely that Jess would send her into actual danger, but the combined force of all the Wilkes stories, which involved madness, mayhem and murder, was distinctly unnerving. But she was not to meet the realities behind the myths; the Wilkes sisters were out. Helen looked doubtfully at the bottles, unsure if it would be safe to leave them; then it occurred to her that if milk bottles were allowed to remain unmolested on doorsteps, so, probably, would be wine bottles. She slotted them neatly into the Wilkes' wire milk-bottle stand, and turned the indicator to 'Two Pints Please'.

As she was unlatching the gate, Richard Pargeter appeared across the road.

"Hang on a minute." He pressed something into her hand. "Heard you asking in the library. This is Dad's, he's lending it to you. Can't stop." It was an impressive-looking copy of *The War of the Worlds*. Touched, she looked up, mouth open to thank him, but he had gone.

Chapter Eight

BEFORE HER NEXT table tennis match, Helen's turn on the umpires' rota came round. She was painfully self-conscious; her stomach churned with nerves, her voice cracked to a whisper, and she twice lost track of the score, distracted by mutters of 'I can't *hear* her.' It was a humiliating experience.

Her own match brought a new problem. David Reeves was popular, mate of Robin Blakely and Andrew Pargeter, generally liked; the Juniors were solidly behind him, hostile to Helen, mate of nobody and not much liked at all. It was like playing against the entire form. She found herself mis-hitting easy shots, and, every time, there was a quiet rustle of pleasure from the spectators. Give me a *chance*, she begged them silently. I can't beat the lot of you together.

"13–7, David's serve," called the umpire.

Thank God she hadn't mentioned anything to Jess about winning the tournament.

"Helen's serve, 10–15."

Joanne Barclay giggled.

Helen stiffened, bounced the ball once, served a blinder. It was the turning point. Ironically, again, it was Joanne who had shown her what to do. She could cope with Joanne. Shut them out, she told herself fiercely. Watch the ball.

She won all five serves. 15 all. David, startled, went to pieces and failed to win another point.

"Game and match to Helen, 21–15." David grinned and shook hands, a cheerful loser. No wonder he was liked.

Mrs. Pargeter came in one day with the news that Mr. Roberts, Lorraine's father, had provided a trophy for the winner, to be kept for a year. The eight survivors' eyes grew starrier. Honour and glory were all very well, but a *trophy*....

Helen had learned something from the David Reeves match. It was quite possible to be beaten by a much inferior player if you were in the wrong frame of mind. You had to focus every atom of your being on winning. And she meant to win, wanted to so badly that it hurt. She lay awake at night, hitting imaginary balls, itching to get on with the next match.

She beat Richard Pargeter easily 21–9—"The seeds are beginning to topple," his mother said gleefully—and still felt that she hadn't yet been stretched to anything like her best.

"It's a good idea, making it a yearly thing," Jess said over the backgammon board, the night before the semifinals. "Everyone works their way up, a better chance of winning every year."

Helen rolled a double four, studied the board carefully before moving. Jess rattled the dice and threw. Three and four. *Blast*, thought Helen, there goes that blot—but Jess missed it, piled another two pieces on to her already crowded six-point. She wasn't playing at all well tonight.

Helen noticed her aunt's face, creased into worry-lines. Surely Jess wasn't old enough to start going wrinkled?

"You're not concentrating, Aunt Jess. Anything the matter?"

"Does it show?" Jess deliberated for a moment. "Look—not a word to anyone about this—I can trust you?—well, we've heard, unofficially, *very* unofficially, there is a possibility that they might be getting ready to wield the axe."

This sounded nasty, but meant nothing to Helen.

"The authorities. Thinking of closing down the school. They're fond of closing things, round here. They'll probably close down Essex, sooner or later, and sell it to the Americans."

"Oh, Aunt *Jess*."

"Yes, well, there may be nothing in it. We had one false alarm a few years ago."

"What would happen?"

"If the school closed? The kids would all have to go into Stambury every day on a special school bus. Mrs. Page—well, she has Mr. Page, earning a very nice salary as a civil engineer. Me, now, I'd be stuck."

Helen began to see what this would mean.

"Couldn't you get another teaching job?"

"More teachers than jobs nowadays. Anyway, I've no car. No public transport worthy of the name. I'd have to move."

It was unthinkable. Jess *belonged* in West Haysham, like frogs belonged in ponds. "But *why*? I mean, it's a *good* school. Everyone's happy there. What do they want to close it down for?"

"Cuts in public spending. Small rural educational establishments are no longer economically viable. Which means, in English, they're giving village schools the chop

67

because they can't afford them. However. Don't look so despairing. Personally, I never believe anything until I see it in black and white, signed, in triplicate. So forget it. Your move."

The subject was firmly closed, and Helen obediently picked the dice up, but the worry-lines were still there.

Helen was miles away during Assembly the next day, lost in private thoughts about the afternoon's match. She was jerked abruptly out of the trance by Mrs. Page saying:

" . . . so to fit in with Mrs. Pargeter, who's a bit tied up this week, we're bringing the final forward to tomorrow morning." Good, thought Helen, the sooner the better. Back in the Juniors room Joanne let out a wail.

"Mrs. Page, it *can't* be tomorrow morning. I've got to go to the hospital to have my plaster off."

"Well, I'm sorry about that, Joanne, but we can't re-arrange our timetable to suit your hospital appoint-ments," Mrs. Page said, unmoved. "If it's a choice between your presence and Mrs. Pargeter's, I think she gets preference, as the tournament was her idea."

Joanne did not look convinced. It could not have suited Helen better. The anti-Helen faction would be as nothing without their leader. She pulled herself up sharply—she hadn't beaten Lorraine yet—but it occurred to her that she was hardly apprehensive at all about the semi-final. She was too confident of winning.

Lorraine looked lost without Joanne. It was like playing against half a person. Helen easily dominated the match by sending everything to Lorraine's backhand, which threw her completely off balance, and coasted home to a 21–10 victory, under the sharp eye of Paul Blakely. He wouldn't be nearly so easy, she thought, set-tling down to watch the second semi-final.

Paul was having an off-day, untypically erratic, but even so never looked like being in trouble; Melanie, who had expected to be slaughtered, was more than relieved to lose only by 21—11, which, against the top seed, was quite respectable.

"I'm *so* sorry I won't be here to watch you win, Paul," Joanne said pointedly. "Be careful not to use the bat *it* used today. It hasn't been fumigated yet." But Paul was as silent as Helen.

"Dark horse," Jess said affectionately that night. "I don't know if I can bear to watch tomorrow."

"I forgot you'd be there."

"There was very nearly a general invitation issued to all parents," Jess said tranquilly, ignoring Helen's horrified expression. "I managed to persuade the two Mrs. P.s that you wouldn't appreciate that, and they were merciful." There was something wrong with this.

"But you could only have known today that I'd *be* in the final."

"Let's say that certain people have been thinking for some time that you might. How d'you rate your chances?"

"Difficult to say," Helen said diplomatically. The trophy was now so near that it was unbearable to think of being beaten. Winning the trophy had assumed a tremendous importance; somehow it would cancel out all the awfulness of the past weeks. To lose, now, would be disaster—she'd be right back to square one. Coming second meant nothing—no title, no trophy. It was winner take all.

"It's largely a matter of psychological warfare," Jess was saying.

"I've found that out already." There was not a lot anyone could tell her about psychological warfare; she felt she was an authority on the subject. "Can I have *War of the Worlds?*" she asked suddenly. This felt right for the occasion.

"You and your Martians. All right. Half."

The book had been a terrible disappointment, much too difficult to read, and Jess, seeing her struggling through the first chapter, had advised her not to bother. "If you force yourself to read it now you'll spoil it for when you're older." So Helen, secretly relieved, had abandoned the book and returned it with polite thanks to Richard, however infuriating it was to be forced to admit that the librarian had actually been right all the time.

It was amazing what a difference the Infants made, streaming in, more than doubling the crowd. "*Quiet!*" Jess was saying. "*Skirt*, Lisa..."

Helen, pulling a face at the Aborigine Boy who glowered back from the wall, was having a bad attack of pre-match nerves. Half an hour and it'll all be over, she told herself, scratching her fingers across the rubber dimples of the bat. Paul was acting Mr. Tough Guy, Mr. Cool, very casual, but she could tell that he was nervous too, underneath. Her eye fell on Jess, leaning against the wall, arms folded. Jess winked. Helen gripped her bat, and winked back.

As the first game of the three-game final got under way it became clear that the finalists were more closely matched than anyone had realised. Helen played steadily; Paul, unsure of his opponent's calibre, was a good deal more cautious than usual. The score reached 15 all, 18 all, 19 all. You could have heard a flea clear its throat. Helen mis-hit the ball into the net, her first unforced error. Game point to Paul, and still his serve... he tried the spin-serve, and Helen, taken by surprise, tapped a weak shot back high over the net. Paul grabbed his chance and smashed. She never got near it.

"First game to Paul, 21–19," said Mrs. Pargeter. "Change ends."

The audience stretched, satisfied with the first game, wanting Paul to win, though the atmosphere was not unfriendly—on the whole feeling was pro-Paul rather than anti-Helen. Jess and Mrs. Page were expressionless. Helen gritted her teeth. You have won the first battle, Paul Blakely, but you have not won the war.

Paul's confidence had been boosted, of course. Helen was still sticking doggedly to her strategy, and forced herself, with some difficulty, to keep playing slightly below her best. She had to take him unawares. Make him think he was going to win.

But it wasn't working like that.

"Twelve-eight, Paul to serve."

He's pulling ahead—I'll never catch up now. Oh, God, I'm going to lose. She knew this with a sudden certainty, a lurch of despair running right through her. She had underestimated Paul, put too much faith in her own stupid tactics.

Then Paul tried another spin-serve. It went so wrong that it didn't hit the table. He tried it again. The ball went in the net. Suddenly seeing a glimmer of hope, Helen moved closer, threatening. Somewhat disconcerted, Paul served a slow, easy ball. Helen slammed it back ferociously. For a second it seemed that it would go wide, but it just caught the edge of the table. Paul hadn't moved.

It had been a lucky shot, and once luck has decided to favour somebody, it continues, most unfairly, to give that person all the breaks. The match, apparently headed for a 2–0 victory to Paul, turned upside down. Helen pulled all the stops out; Paul lost the rhythm of the game and began to make mistakes.

"Game to Helen, 21–14." Mrs. Pargeter was as enthralled as anyone by the sudden turn of events.

Helen had the advantage now, and she knew it. The very fact of being beaten was upsetting Paul—he simply wasn't used to it. Seeing that the game was moving beyond his grasp, that the only hope of retaining some dignity was to turn the whole thing into a joke, to show that he didn't care at *all*, he began to play the fool, shouting "Foot fault!" grinning at the appreciative onlookers. Helen stood placidly through the clowning and romped home to a fine win, 21–9 in the deciding game.

"Congratulations, both of you," Mrs. Pargeter said, shaking hands. "Most entertaining." Paul gave a silly grin and a not-caring shrug, ha-ha, only a game, see what a good sport I am. "Until that last game," she added sternly. "I don't know what came over you, young man."

Victory was glorious—Helen beamed round at everyone, in a happy daze. Mrs. Page patted her on the back. "Mr. Roberts is coming round at half-past three to do the honours in person, Helen. You can gaze at the trophy in anticipation all afternoon."

It wasn't quite the same as the Duke of Kent—had anyone thought to *ask* the Duke of Kent?—but a public presentation . . . wait till Mum heard about this.

But after lunch Joanne Barclay returned, deplastered, arm in a sling, and on hearing the news went into a long conference with Lorraine.

"Chairs round," Mrs. Page said, when the Juniors had all drifted in on hearing the afternoon bell. "Television. It's not half term yet, let's try and get *some*thing done . . ." The television warmed up slowly to show a clock eating away the seconds of the final minute before the programme. It was *Getting the Message*, a series about communications which Helen normally found absorbing; today's edition, *Propaganda and Distorting the Truth*, was no exception, although on every newspaper she saw the headline 'Helen Keates Storms to Championship Victory' which was hardly distorting the truth at all.

"You can do some painting for the rest of the afternoon," Mrs. Page said afterwards, sensing that the form was still too restless for the intelligent discussion on newspapers which she had optimistically planned.

Helen, still in her benevolent mood, settled down with paper and pencil to do the outlines of her picture. Not artistically gifted, she was doing a reproduction of the Underwater Scene which she had managed to stretch to fill seven Art lessons at Craddock House. Mistakes could easily be painted over and turned into exotic aquatic creatures, or, in extreme cases, into part of the sea. She could see herself doing it again next year at the Comprehensive.

"You're not really the champion, Mole," said Joanne.

Carry on, you unplastered ugly. There's not a thing you can do about it. Bitch to your nasty little heart's content.

"You haven't beaten everyone in the school. You haven't beaten me."

Too bad, flower, you should take more care and not fall off horses. Helen considered drawing a plug and socket on the end of her electric eel, decided this was going too far, contented herself with a few sparks.

"You've got to play me, Mole."

"But, Joanne, your arm." Beverley looked at the sling with concern.

"Left-handed. Well, Mole?"

"No."

"You're *afraid*. You're afraid you'll lose, Mole." Her face was etched with hate. Helen's bubble of happiness

73

was shattered. She would have to play Joanne. She knew it. Oh, damn and hell. *And* bloody.

"I'm not afraid. I'll play."

Joanne nodded, satisfied. "Tomorrow, lunchtime. Lorraine will umpire..."

"I'm not playing if Lorraine umpires."

"That wouldn't be fair, Joanne," Melanie said. "You can't expect her to."

"All right then, Melanie can be umpire. I suppose you need all the help you can get."

The final timbers of her new-found status creaked and collapsed. It was quite true—she wasn't a rightful champion unless she could beat anyone in the school, Joanne included. When Mr. Roberts, tall and genial, arrived to present her with the trophy, she almost pushed it back at him. It wasn't hers yet. She had to win it all over again tomorrow.

Chapter Nine

HELEN, SITTING BY the window, had the expression of one who is trying to choose between death by hanging and the electric chair. Nobody could have looked less like a champion, newly victorious.

Jess had been bemused when her niece had trailed in, feet dragging, and deposited her trophy right at the back of the dresser shelf. She had planted herself in the chair by the window as soon as tea was over, and all Jess's attempts at conversation had been met with monosyllables. Jess was puzzled and disappointed; giving up, she had gone about her own business, fetching down two demijohns of wine for racking. This was normally an intriguing business, involving chemicals, filters and lengths of plastic tubing, like a mad scientist's laboratory; today Helen appeared not to notice.

Could she possibly beat Joanne? Could she even *play*, with her left hand? She could hear Richard's voice saying 'David won', but wasn't she, Helen, the champion, now Goliath? Wasn't Joanne, injured, more of a David? And David won...

"Fold me a filter paper, would you, Helen?"

Helen sighed. "I suppose so."

"Thank you *very* much, I'll do it myself. What *is* the matter with you?" she asked, a new note in her voice.

"Oh, leave me alone."

"Right! That is *it*. No, you stay right there where you are. I've got a few things to say to you. Have you ever *once* thought of anybody but yourself? Well, start now. Has it ever occurred to you, wallowing away in your little sea of self-pity, that I've made quite a few sacrifices to have you here? That perhaps other people have problems too? I didn't mind. I was glad of the chance to get to know you. Now I'm starting to wonder if you're worth getting to know."

Helen, aghast—was the world ending?—cowered against the wall.

"And don't shrink away from me like that! I'm not going to hit you, for Heaven's sake, though to look at you anyone would think I whipped you every morning. I've put up with your miseries, your silences, for weeks now. You mope around, you won't make friends, you never go out—I've been patient, done my best to cheer you up, left you to brood, I've tried everything. And what do you give in return? Nothing. Too wrapped up in yourself. The one time I asked some friends round, you went to bed at eight o'clock. So, right, Helen's shy, I'll spare her, no more visitors. Do you really think I normally stay in every evening? And I was looking forward to you coming. Are you so unhappy, staying with me? Am I such a rotten hostess?"

Helen was trembling violently; with a sudden gulp she ran from the room, stumbling upstairs to throw herself on to her bed and cry herself sick.

"Oh, *damn*," said Jess.

Helen had dozed off some time after midnight, eyes burning, head throbbing, nose sniffly, only to be tormented by vivid, ghoulish dreams, and the morning, with Jess pale, haggard and silent, was like a continuation of the nightmares. The left-handed game had become curiously unimportant—beside last night it seemed a triviality. She wasn't worth getting to know. She was ruining Jess's life, stopping her from having friends. Jess hated her. How could anything else matter?

And from the first shot of the game it was obvious that she would not win. She was outclassed. Her left hand wouldn't play at all—it was as much as she could manage to get the ball back over the net. One glance at Joanne's face told her that she had been practising. Almost certainly she had been practising for this very match ever since the day she'd first seen Helen play. If Helen should win, she could not refuse this challenge. Not with honour. And now there was no honour left; there was nothing.

It was the worst day of her life. Before the afternoon's lessons she went up to Mrs. Page and spoke to her in a low voice.

"I've never heard such nonsense in my life," Mrs. Page said sharply. "Any private business between you and Joanne can hardly affect the Tournament result. Don't be so silly, Helen. I'd thought better of you."

Helen almost shrugged, but remembered just in time about Mrs. Page's views on cheek. Her depression was as blinding as her euphoria had been only twenty-four hours earlier. If you were more unhappy than this, she thought, you would be dead.

Mrs. Page told them to finish their paintings. It was an effort to move, but Mrs. Page must not be provoked, so, moving like a sleepwalker, she collected water, paint and palette. As a rule she enjoyed mixing paint, adding the water drop by drop to the powder, watching it change to a lumpy paste, then to a smooth, thick liquid. Today she just

77

sloshed water into the blue and mechanically set about producing a vaguely sea-like green.

Joanne, gloating and triumphant, had organized a joke-telling session, as if to emphasize Helen's defeat.

"Mummy, mummy, what's a werewolf?" asked Lorraine. "Keep still, dear, while I'm trying to comb your face."

Paul grinned. "D'you hear about the Irish firing squad? They stood in a circle." Beverley did not understand this, and it had to be explained to her.

"What do one-parent families eat for breakfast?" said Joanne, staring at Helen. "Snap, crackle and no pop." Her audience, aware that this was loaded, was silent. "Some people's fathers will do anything to get away from them. They run off with other women."

Oh, God, strike her dead. Destroy her. Like you did with Sodom and Gomorrah. Make it slow and painful.

"Other people never know who their father is at all. There's a word for that. It's called illegitimate. It means you're a little bastard."

Helen stood up, taking her palette in one hand and her water jar in the other, walked round the table and upturned the palette over Joanne's head. Startled, Joanne opened her mouth to shout, just in time to receive the full blast of water which Helen emptied on her.

"My father's dead," Helen said mildly, watching multicoloured rivers of paint flow through Joanne's hair, down past her mouth which was choking on watery magenta, flooding down to soak her once-white blouse. Then she thought: "Mrs. Page will explode at me. I can't take that"—and, turning, walked from the room.

She was half-way down the road when she heard a voice frantically shouting her name. Jess. Helen stopped and walked slowly back, responding automatically to authority. She steeled herself, but her aunt only said: "Oh, *Helen*," took her by the arm and led her back indoors. After rubbing her head distractedly for a moment, under the interested scrutiny of the Infants, she left Helen in the office, and went to confer with Mrs. Page.

Helen eyed a piece of potato, dropped at lunch and overlooked. Idly, she wondered what they would do with her. Probably she would end up in Care, later there would be Borstal—it would be sad for Mum, who would weep buckets and blame herself, but this could not be helped. Every time she thought of Joanne Barclay, ridiculous and gasping, it would be worth every second of Borstal. She was glad she'd done it. She didn't care.

Mrs. Page hadn't exploded. In fact, she wasn't at all sure what to do. Jess was sent to talk to Helen, but emerged no wiser.

"What *can* have happened?" Mrs. Page mused; she had found the top group equally unhelpful, all interrogation being met with a conspiracy of silence. At this point Mrs. Barclay arrived, having been summoned by telephone. Interrupting Mrs. Page's apologies, she said briskly: "Don't worry, I'll get it out of her," and bore her freshly tinted daughter off home to be washed and changed.

Half an hour later, Jess returned to the office.

"Well, you awful child, next time you do something like this, let us know first. Then we can all come and watch."

This was not pre-Borstal talk; Helen blinked in confusion.

"Under the circumstances, Mrs. Barclay has decided not to press charges, which means you're not actually to be flogged, just given a telling off, which is what I'm supposed to be doing now."

"You *know* . . . what she said? Who told?"

"Joanne told her mother."

79

"*Joanne* did?"

"Indeed she did. If you knew Mrs. Barclay, you would understand why. She's just been on the phone, pleading on your behalf."

(What Mrs. Barclay had in fact said was: "She's played me up that much lately, Mrs. Page, with no horses and whatever, giving her a coat of paint is *nothing* compared to what I've been tempted to do. If it quietens her down a bit, that Helen will have done me a favour.")

"Will I have to apologize? Because I'm not sorry."

"I'm sure you're not. I should think you enjoyed every second of it. I would have. Oh, Lord. I'm the one who should be apologizing. Helen, I'm sorry I was so beastly last night. I'm worried, as you know, but that's no excuse for taking it out on you. Friends?"

"Friends. And Aunt Jess—I'm sorry too. For everything. Definitely friends." She stood up and solemnly shook Jess's hand. It took a major effort of will not to start crying again.

That seemed to be the end of it, but in the evening, Helen, answering the doorbell, was somewhat alarmed to find Mrs. Barclay, together with Joanne, hair still slightly greenish, on the step.

"Joanne has come to apologize." Mrs. Barclay jabbed her daughter menacingly in the back.

"Er ... come in," Helen said. It seemed to be turning into a day of apologies, and this one would not be pleasant. But this was not the Joanne she knew and loathed; she looked subdued, pale, as if one of her skins had been scrubbed off during the cleaning process.

"I'm sorry. I shouldn't have said that—you know."

"It's all right," Helen said quickly, not wanting to prolong this. "I asked if you could have the trophy. Mrs. Page said no."

80

"I don't want it," Joanne said, surprisingly. "It's yours. When they give us a left-handed trophy, I'll have that." It felt unreal, standing in Jess's hall holding this too-polite conversation with Joanne Barclay. Joanne-with-Mrs. Barclay seemed to become as insubstantial as Lorraine-with-Joanne, as if what people were depended largely on who they were with at the time.

"That's amazing," Helen reflected aloud, after they had gone. "She looked *squashed*. I reckon she'll be all right now."

"I should hope so. You've put up with enough."

"You *know*? You *know* what she's been like to me this term?"

"Yes, of course. Mrs. Page and Mrs. Pargeter too. I did try to explain why, that you shouldn't take it personally . . ."

Helen was gazing at her with wordless accusation.

"No, don't look at me like that. We *couldn't* interfere. You had to sort it out yourselves. If someone had said to Joanne: 'Leave poor Helen alone, you're upsetting her', she'd have been even worse. She'd never have respected you. You had to stand up for yourself. Although we hadn't anticipated that you might go about it *quite* so dramatically."

"It's a funny world if you have to dye somebody green to make them respect you."

"A very profound remark. Mind you, it wasn't such a bad idea. She can be a proper little punk, Joanne Barclay; she might as well have the green hair to go with it."

Chapter Ten

>⟶ ❀ ❀ ⟵

"'WOULD IT BE possible for Helen to come here for half term?'" Jess read, poker-faced. "'I would so love to see her, and Alison has a beautiful room. . . .'"

Helen nearly choked on her Sugar Puffs.

"I know Alison's beautiful rooms. Mum took me to her house in Richmond once, before she moved. She hardly let me *breathe*. It was 'be careful of the stereo' . . . 'mind your sticky fingers on the chair'—they *weren't* sticky—'don't touch that' . . . I went out and sat in the garden in the end. For *two hours*. That Alison, she doesn't think children are human. She'd stand me in the hall and hang coats on me."

"Dear, dear. I don't think, as a concerned aunt, I could allow that. So it's no?"

"It's no," Helen said. It would have been marvellous to see Mum, but Alison . . . and she was going to the cinema in Stambury with the Pargeters on Saturday . . . "Absolutely no."

After the paint incident Helen had found herself something of a celebrity among the Juniors, who had never seen anything quite like it, and even more so with the Infants, who had received the story at second- and third-hand, by which time some versions had Helen throwing paint bombs at the entire room, Mrs. Page included.

Joanne, still perceptibly emerald about the head, was civil but awkward. Realizing that the ball was now in her court, Helen made a courteous enquiry about Joanne's arm, which brought forth a discourse from Lorraine on how the man at the hospital had never in his life seen an arm heal so well after a compound fracture. It was easy to take the conversation from there and by lunch-time, incredibly, Helen and the rest of the group were chatting in quite a normal way. Melanie tentatively suggested to Helen that they walk home together, and it was while they were passing the church, which Helen privately called 'The Fishery' because of the poster outside which seemed, from a distance, to say 'Cod is Good,' that Mrs. Pargeter pulled up beside them to invite Helen out.

"I meant to ask you before, but I've had to rest a lot lately"—this was true, she'd hardly been in school at all for a while. "We'll pick you up at one thirty. Stay to tea," she added.

Helen felt an unexpected sense of belonging when they piled out of the car at Long Acre on Saturday. Simply knowing the way to the kitchen and the bathroom, not needing to be told "This way, Helen"—it made a tremendous difference.

"Was he good, Jon?" Mrs. Pargeter asked, scooping her youngest up from the floor. Jonathan had been left at home—'looking after Dad', Andrew said.

"He said I was marvellous," Mr. Pargeter said. "I played so quietly all afternoon he hardly knew I was there. He's letting me have boiled egg and soldiers for tea."

Tea finished, Andrew settled down to a game of chess with his father, and Michael and Richard went to try Michael's newly-constructed kite out on the playing fields, taking Helen with them. "I expect you'll be going straight home," Mrs. Pargeter said, "so I'll say goodbye now. You must start to come round in the evenings and watch television with us. I'm sadly outnumbered by all these men."

Michael, kite in hand, ran on ahead, darting and swooping. Richard, following at a more leisurely pace by Helen's side, said casually:

"I wonder if it will be a girl this time."

"Who will?"

"The baby. Didn't you know? I didn't think it was a secret. She's having another one in December."

But she's only just had one!—Helen almost said, realized in time that this was not quite the right response, and changed it to: "Good heavens. How lovely."

"Elizabeth Louise, if it manages to be a her. I was going to be Elizabeth Louise. We all were. She doesn't seem to want to come."

So there was something that didn't necessarily obey Mrs. Pargeter after all.

The playing fields were vast, especially for such a small village, and the sunny evening had brought the children out. They kicked balls, ran, swung, crowded with interest around Michael and his kite.

"We come up here most evenings when it's fine," Richard told her. "You want to come too." For once, he was right; she did. She soon slipped into the playing-field crowd, and Jess told her kindly that she was glad to see the back of her for a change. In a corner of the field stood a row of swings, paint flaking and cracked; next to them an ancient wooden seesaw creaked grudgingly up and down. Finding Melanie Davies perched on one of the swings one evening, Helen sat down on the next, and they began to chat pleasantly, pushing to and fro with their feet. This became a habit with them in the quiet hours after the smaller children had been taken, protesting, home to bed. As they looked out over that expanse of green, civilization could have been a million miles away—it was enchanted.

"This is beautiful," Helen remarked on the last evening before school re-opened.

"What is?" Melanie asked, buttoning up the too-big blue cardigan she wore to keep out the mild chill of the evening breeze. "Being in the country, after London?"

"No, it's not that exactly." It was a blend of things: the countryside, the newly-found, undemanding companionship of Melanie, the peace with Joanne, the sheer transience of these unrepeatable short months, the middle of the sandwich... "It's mostly because it won't last. London's lovely too, you know, only different. It's *because* it's so different. I wouldn't want to stay here always."

"I do," Melanie said.

"What, even when you're grown up? What *do* you want to do?"

"Just the usual—get married, have a nice house, children..."

"And that's *all*?" Helen had never even thought of getting married, except once, to Prince Edward, and she'd grown out of him *years* ago. A husband might have a terrible surname, and Helen was fussy about names. It might be Bott. She had a great horror of the name Bott.

"That's all most people want really, isn't it?" Melanie was saying. Helen thought briefly of Deborah, who was going to be an astronaut. Women's Liberation would meet its match in Melanie.

The weather, as if bored by its own monotony, had done an about-turn—it was all blue skies and sunshine now. Everyone longed to be outdoors, but Mrs. Page was merciless.

"This is exactly the time of year you'll find yourselves doing exams at the Chase, so I'll have no excuses, thank you. Helen, come over here, please, I want a word."

Helen obeyed, curious rather than apprehensive. Mrs. Page was in a good mood.

"Now, young lady, what in the world am I to do with you? You're not being stretched, Helen. You're a bright girl, coming from a school with an exceptional academic standard—you must realise that the work I've been giving you is too easy."

Helen could think of nothing that could, with modesty, be said to that.

"I was wondering if we could find you some special project—it would be a better use of your time. Got any particular interest, hobby, something you'd like to try? Nothing come to mind? Well, don't worry, go away and think about it."

"You weren't long," Beverley said as she sat down.

"About five foot one and a half, same as always," she answered neatly. Beverley, aware of the new order of things, had rapidly dropped her allegiance to Joanne. However, with Helen now a respected member of the community, and proving herself to have a pretty sharp line of wit, the butt of everyone's jokes and ill-temper was once more firmly Beverley. Even Helen found herself joining in—Beverley was so *irritating*. As for Joanne—well, out of school, apparently, Joanne was more bullied than bully. Heavens above, she'd almost felt sorry for her. Joanne was a different matter altogether, now that she'd seen both sides of her, heads and tails.

Beverley sniffed and retreated behind her *Teen-Dream* magazine. They had all been told to bring along a magazine or periodical—"That does *not* include the *Beano*"—as a follow-up to one of the 'Getting the

Message' programmes. In theory, they were comparing and discussing; in fact, they were reading the juicy bits.

"This is good," Beverley was saying. "Your Horoscope Profile." Beverley seemed possessed of a morbid urge to reveal her own character. "It's got me just right. Listen. Gemini. You are lively, quick-witted and alert, intelligent and comm ... comm ... oh, I can't read that word. Anyway, it's very true. It's accurate. Dad says I'm his bright little button."

Paul spluttered. "It's the right sign, anyway, Ten-Ton. Gemini the Twins. You'd make two of anybody." A wasp buzzed over in their direction; Beverley yelped, and waved *Teen-Dream* at it. "Leave it *alone*," Paul said. "It doesn't want you, it doesn't know where you've been. Stupid women."

"That's rubbish, what you've got," said Joanne, who was skimming disdainfully through *Woman's Friend*. "So's this. It's awful. I don't know why Mum gets them. The Problem Page is the best, and I'm not allowed to read that. She's torn it out. I've got a problem mother."

"I know those," Paul said. "I read the covers. Always a miracle baby. The Baby that Should Never Have Been Born, My Baby's Fight to Live. Sometimes they have a bonanza week, My Miracle Triplets, Exclusive by a mother with a wooden leg."

Helen swopped her *Observer Supplement* for Melanie's *Gardening Today*. It was a pity Jess wasn't more daring with papers and magazines. The *Observer Supplement* didn't even have a Problem Page to be ripped out. All Jess ever took was the *Telegraph* except on Sundays when she had the *Observer* and the *News of the World* as well. She called this sampling both ends of the spectrum.

David Reeves killed the wasp, was cheered, began to cut

it up with a penknife. "Put that in the bin!" roared Mrs. Page. Helen exchanged *Gardening Today* for *Teen-Dream*. She thought it was terrible. Your Fella's Character Revealed in his Ears. How to Make Boys Notice you. Super Competition—You Can Win Rod Stewart's Sock. *She* could write a better magazine than this. She could write . . .

"Very good idea," Jess said. "Tremendous initiative, Mrs. Pargeter would say."

Helen, still a little damp after her bath, was already having her doubts. To start a school magazine had been a brilliant idea; actually working out how to go about it was another matter. She was quite clear as to what it would *not* contain, but no alternatives sprang to mind.

"Well, what would you want to read in it?" asked Jess. "Think what you find most interesting in papers and magazines." Helen fetched an exercise book and a biro.

"Book reviews, television reviews," she read out after a while. "Interesting local events. Letters page."

"Don't forget Editorial Comments. That's you. Your chance to tell the world your deepest thoughts. And remember your readership. What would the rest of the school be interested in?"

Reluctantly, Helen wrote: Horoscopes, Horses, Football. "I hope they won't all do horsy book reviews."

"I know," said Jess, who was in on the joke. "*Suzy Goes to the Knackers* and *I was a Teenage Palomino*. Get Joanne to write about her accident. She'll love that."

Joanne proved more than willing to do this. Indeed, the whole school, enchanted by the idea of seeing their names in print, were unexpectedly enthusiastic about providing articles. Mrs. Page decided to make Monday afternoons Magazine Afternoons, and suggested that Helen could do with an assistant. After some thought, she asked Richard Pargeter, who accepted, loftily ignoring the giggles of 'who's got a girlfriend, then.' When you were Richard Pargeter you could afford to be above such things.

It was all very convenient. Helen was already going to the Pargeters a couple of times a week to watch television, and now Editor and Assistant Editor appointed book reviewers, made lists, examined contributions, pondered whether a report on a Brownies' meeting would be of general interest.

Helen pinned up notices in both form rooms: 'All letters to the Editors will be welcomed if legible.' When in the Infants room she was struck once more by the devotion of the small children to her aunt, who knew the name of every pet rabbit, every baby sister, who noticed the misery of Sherrilyn Comfort, victim of unrequited love, and made her Form Prefect. It was outrageous that this could be abruptly ended, the Infants shuttled off to Stambury, just by the stroke of a pen. It was unthinkable that Lisa should not have Jess's skirt to pull. And the worst of it was knowing that this might happen, and being powerless to lift a finger to stop it. She couldn't even *talk* about it, except to Jess, who didn't often want to talk about it. Given half a chance, Helen would have got the whole school picketing the Minister of Education in Westminster. Alone, she could only worry.

Chapter Eleven

⇒ ❊ ❊ ⇐

THEY WERE MAGICAL days, tinted gold by the rays of the sun. It seemed that nothing had ever been so perfect. Helen bustled around happily, no longer 'the new girl' but 'the Magazine Editor'. The Wimbledon Championships began and the television was on all afternoon, an annual tradition and treat. Then the evenings—debates with Richard, putting away vast quantities of Coke in the Pargeters' garden; leisurely chats on the swings with Melanie, probing the possibility of the coming Pargeter baby turning out to be twins, Elizabeth *and* Louise, in one fell swoop.

"This magazine is going to be one of the literary land-marks of modern times," Jess said. "You'll have to sell the film rights. *West Haysham School Magazine*, the movie they said they'd never dare to make."

Helen was industriously copying the horoscope page from an old *Daily Mirror*, altering 'wages' to 'pocket money' and 'your partner' to 'your parents'.

"That is *plagiarism*," Jess said, stopping to look.

"I wondered what the word for it was," Helen said, without looking up. "I thought there probably was one. But I'm changing the signs round. I've put the Virgo horoscope under Leo and Libra under Virgo. Moving them all up one."

"You've got a great future as an astrologer," Jess said, amused. "I always suspected that was how they did it. When are you going to get that editorial done?"

Helen sighed. The editorial was turning out to be a lot more difficult than she had foreseen. The obvious subject—'Why we must keep our school open'—could not be used.

"I particularly hope to have the magazine out by Monday," Jess went on. "School inspector's coming. He'd be most interested in a school magazine. So press on."

Helen sat back, digesting this. Then it sank in—a school inspector, coming to pass the verdict on the school. This was the man who was going to do the axe-wielding and giving-the-chop. If the magazine made a good impression, it might just tilt the balance in their favour . . .

"He's likely to look at the magazine, Aunt Jess?"

"Almost certain to."

But he might just read the front page. She had intended this to feature 'Joanne Barclay (13) Breaks Arm in Three Places in Dramatic Accident' but this would now have to go on Page Two. On Page One would be Helen's editorial.

Jess roared with laughter when she read it.

"Oh, Helen! This is amazing stuff. No, no, I'm not criticising, I love it . . . 'coming from the city I was amazed at the difference a small village school makes to your life. It is wonderful to see children healthy and happy after only a few minutes' travel, after watching my old schoolfriends stumble in every morning, tired and weak from long journeys, coughing on traffic fumes, squashed into classrooms so overcrowded that we couldn't move without knocking each other over . . . clearly if everyone in Britain went to a village school we would all grow up stronger and better educated . . .' I appreciate the sentiments, but I'd love to see the Head of Craddock House's face if she read this."

"It's called Propaganda and Distorting the Truth," Helen said happily. "We had a programme about it."

"I don't think the idea was that you should start *doing* it . . . Good Lord, there's a series next year called *Crime and Punishment*." Jess's voice trailed away as she considered the implications. But Helen was quite satisfied with her aunt's reaction. This, clearly, was just what was needed.

"A historic moment," Jess said, wiping her hands. Helen and Richard had watched, enthralled, as a series of Page Ones rolled off the duplicating machine. "Right, Page Two coming up. You'll need the stapler, to fasten the pages together."

It was a hit—a sell-out. The whole village seemed to want to read it. They had to print fifty more. Every page was scanned and fingered, from Helen's Editorial on the front page to the Sports on the back—'First Annual Table Tennis Tournament—on-the-spot report by our Sports Correspondent, Paul Blakely (13)'. Beverley thought her horoscope very accurate, which was remarkable, considering it was the Cancer forecast for June 5th, four weeks before. Joanne, never having known she was lined up for the front page, was delighted to be on the second. Helen was radiant, drunk with success and congratulation.

Then the Inspector called.

He was a plump, smiling man, hot and sweaty in his brown suit. Ridiculous, to dress like that in July, thought Helen—he was obviously a stupid sort of man, which was a bad omen . . . And she didn't trust that smile. It didn't mean a thing; he smiled all the time, at everything. She envied the others their ignorance, not knowing how much depended on his visit.

After talking to Mrs. Page for what seemed like hours—buzz, buzz, Helen couldn't catch a word of it—he sat in a corner to watch them, spilling out over the sides of the small school chair. This was worse than anything. It was like performing in an unfinished play, while the author watches from the wings and decides what to do with the characters in the last act. The whole form was unnaturally quiet. Nobody liked being watched. They were all very glad when he moved on to the Infants' room.

So he wasn't going to look at the magazine after all. But, having observed the Infants, he returned, still smiling, picked up a copy, smiled at it, asked to meet the Editor, smiled at Helen. He appeared to read the editorial, but made no comment. Helen was no wiser. Nor did Jess have much to say on the subject, merely remarking that inspectors were a necessary evil, and thank heavens *that* was over. About the likely fate of the school, nothing.

The days were beginning to slip past rather too quickly for Helen's liking. Each individual day passed slowly, as if stretched to its very limits, but then, wham, suddenly a whole week had gone by. Time played funny tricks, she reflected over tea. Only two weeks of term-time left. Just long enough to get one more edition of the magazine done. And then? Lost in thought, she twirled the tomato sauce to four o'clock.

"I won't say 'a penny for your thoughts'," Jess said, in between mouthfuls of omelette. "They look as if they're worth a good deal more than that."

"Five pence, to you."

"You drive a hard bargain, Miss Keates."

"Cash on delivery."

Jess got up, shaking her head. "Robbing a poor teacher of her last five p. in the world. There you are. Now, after all that, it had better be good. Discovered the meaning of life?"

"Not quite. I was just thinking, you know, term's nearly over, I'll be going back home, then there's the Comprehensive..."

"Scared?"

"That's what's so odd. I'm not, not really. It can't be much worse than it was here, at first. And there won't be any Joanne ... at least, there might be someone like her, but I wouldn't be me. I mean, I wouldn't be the me I was then, so it wouldn't..." she gave up, her meaning tied in knots. Jess seemed to understand anyway.

"You only get one Joanne in your life, and you've had yours."

"That's it. And *everyone* will be new. And Deborah's going there too. I reckon it'll be O.K."

"Very sensible. Good Lord, Helen, you're a different girl. When you first came you were a quivering wreck, half the time. And look at you now. You're a success story. You win the Trophy. Every team you're put in zooms to the top of the lists. You edit and publish a best-selling magazine. The only thing you can't do is art, and even then you discover a completely new use for paint. Heaven knows what you'll do at the Comprehensive. You've got the world at your feet."

Helen was used to thinking of herself as appallingly ordinary, but, put like that, it did sound a rather impressive list. If only it ended with: 'and you saved the school from closing'...

The doorbell rang.

"It's Mrs. Simmons, Helen," Jess called. "Phone call for me. Won't be long." She returned, ten minutes later, looking exasperated and amused at the same time.

"I'm going senile. I read it in the paper and it never occurred to me ... Look." She pushed the *News of the World* to Helen.

"'I Blame Concorde, says Runaway Vicar's Wife'," Helen read.

"Not that, birdbrain. Underneath."

"'Major Flooding Hits the West Country' ... oh!"

"Exactly. Unbelievable though it may seem to us, basking in our heat wave. They were evacuated this morning. Alison's ground floor is under eighteen inches of water, Barbara said."

Alison's beautiful house, beautiful no longer. It was like a judgment.

"It's crazy. We've had such lovely weather."

"Well, the last few days it's been pouring in Devon and Cornwall and so—floods. We had ours in the spring, here in the east."

"So Mum won't be staying with Alison any longer?"

"Obviously not. She expects to arrive here tomorrow evening."

After school on Monday, Jess called a conference.

"What's she eating at the moment? Get *off* that, Logan. Off!"

Helen cast her mind back. "Absolutely nothing fried, that's deadly, clogs up your arteries. Yogurt, pots and pots of yogurt. Honey. Horrible bran, like sawdust. Fruit."

"I remember now, the last time you came down it was diet-everything. Diet-bread, diet-butter—diet-flavour shampoo, I wouldn't be surprised. But now she might even need fattening up. It's so difficult to know. Does she eat salads?"

"All the time."

"Right. I'll go brandishing a bottle of rhubarb and coax emergency supplies out of Dorothy Pargeter. You take my purse and scour the supermarket. Use your discretion. Mission understood?"

"Yes, Sergeant-Major. Synchronize watches. Roger and out."

Jess threw a pot-holder at her; she ducked, and fled.

The mini-mini-supermarket was empty but for Helen and a girl sitting chewing at the checkout. 'Slimers Spread' said the hand-written notice in the dairy food freezer. It was amazing how grown-ups went on at you about spelling, when they couldn't do it themselves.

The checkout-girl, who had been watching her with suspicion—the manager was hot on kiddy shoplifters—began mechanically to ring up the purchases. A sign behind her read: 'Checkouts opperators only will serve cigarettes'.

"Does that mean that only you serve cigarettes, or that you don't serve anything else?" Helen asked.

"Don't give me that," said the girl through a mouthful of gum. "You know quite well you're too young for fags. That's one pound eighty-five. Kids!" she muttered. She must have been all of seventeen.

Jess sent Helen up to the playing fields. "What with train, bus and taxi, I doubt if we'll see Barbara before nine." Helen got there just in time to join in a version of Hide and Seek which involved swinging over a ditch on a rope to get Home. This occupied her mind fully, but later, during the ritual natter with Melanie, she began to realize the news potential of her mother's escapade—a terrific headline: 'Editor's Mother (over 21) Rescued from Drowning in Dangerous Adventure'.

"I saw that on the evening news," Melanie said. "Furniture floating down the street, men carrying women out of houses. I didn't see your Mum, though. No, that's a stupid thing to say. I might have. I wouldn't have known if I did."

Mum the television star. Melanie was wearing a deep-pink cardigan today, even bigger than the blue one.

"Pink's a lovely word," Helen said. "Not the colour, just the word. Like egg. That's a perfect word, it *sounds* like an egg. It's a pity they both have to be Beverley Simmons. She's egg-shaped *and* pink."

"Pink?"

"Pink. And Joanne's bright red; Paul's dark grey. Lorraine's a sort of watery olive green."

She had worked this out now. People changed exactly like their colours did—by contrast, highlighting them or toning them down. A subdued colour, like watery-green Lorraine, could almost be blotted out altogether. An orange person in a group of greens and blues would be the centre of attention; put him with reds and yellows and he'd melt into anonymity. This was why Michael, the only red Pargeter, was much more conspicuous at home, with his cool-coloured family, than at school. She intended to write a book one day, explaining all this. The book would have to be carefully phrased. Once she had said absent-mindedly to Jess: "I wonder what colour the new Pargeter baby will be", which had produced an interesting reaction.

"What am I?" Melanie asked.

"Royal blue." Melanie was satisfied with this, inter-preting it as a compliment, which indeed it was. That was the great thing about Melanie—she accepted the most obscure remarks as pearls of wisdom.

"You'd better go, if you want to meet your Mum. That was the church bell, it's half-past eight."

Helen pushed herself up high and leapt off, landing

squarely on both feet. Waving, she broke into a run. There would be just enough time to wash and change, if she got a move on.

But there was not. Opening the back door, she heard voices—Jess's low buzz, and a higher one, which crashed abruptly back into her memory.

Her mother was early.

Chapter Twelve

"MY DARLING! Come to Mummy!"—and before she had time to blink Helen was swept into a violent hug which went on and on and on, until she badly wanted to wriggle.

She had every reason to blink. Her mother looked—she looked the same person but a different version, as if the makers had decided to call her in and put out a new model. The sleek hair had been transformed into a mass of curls. The smart brown trouser suit was unknown to Helen. And nobody could have looked less like a recuperating convalescent. Mum was positively blooming, pink-cheeked and—she glanced at the hips (Mum always said everything went straight to her hips)—almost certainly on a diet. The ash-tray beside her contained two cigarette ends, and a third was balanced on the rim, still smoulder-ing. At least it wasn't one of the giving-up-smoking times. These were never easy.

Her mother was looking at her, too—hard.

"Darling, you're *filthy*. Your legs, they're all scratched. And what's that red patch on your arm? What *have* you been doing?"

"Just a gnat bite, where I've been scratching it, that's all. We've been swinging over a ravine on a rope, it's terrific fun..."

"You've been *what*?" It was a squeal, sounding, it suddenly occurred to Helen, uncomfortably like Alison, the time Helen had inadvertently picked up a piece of her Wedgwood.

"Don't worry," said Jess, from the sidelines, detached. "It's a very small ravine and a very strong rope. She's getting plenty of exercise."

"I see. So you've taken to rough games, darling. Mummy was a little hurt that you weren't here to meet her. Oh, come here, let me look at you again ... have you missed me?"

Helen reassured this almost-Mum, of course she had. Why hadn't Helen written longer letters?

"There wasn't much to say ... and then I was so busy with the magazine ..."

"Tell me *all about* the magazine."

Mum wanted to be told *all about* everything. Even when Helen had run out of things to tell, she sat expectantly, waiting for more. My mouth aches, Helen thought. I've got tongue fatigue.

Her mother, too, had much to tell, though the evacuation episode was a sad let-down; there had been no last-minute snatching from the jaws of a watery death.

"No, we had just enough warning to get out in time—Alison took what she could, but the *damage*—thousands of pounds—thank heavens she's insured. Alison's a survivor. She survived a broken marriage, after all." There didn't seem much else you could do with a broken marriage, except shoot yourself. Her mother peered at her watch. "It's nearly ten. Darling, you should be in bed, you'll be dead in the morning, and it's school—I won't be long either, Mummy's very tired ..."

"Is she?" Helen nearly said. She wondered if her mother

had always called herself 'Mummy' like this, as if she was talking about someone else—she supposed so, but she'd never really noticed before . . .

It wasn't until the next evening that she began to feel that things were somehow not quite right. It was lovely to have Mum here, but it seemed to change the atmosphere. It was more than the fug of cigarette smoke. The evening was beautifully sunny, beckoning Helen outside, but her mother said reproachfully: "Darling, I haven't *seen* you for two months," and she had to stay, though really they had done almost two months' worth of talking the night before. Mum chattered on—"I want to know *everything* you did in school today"—but when she asked to see one of Helen's exercise books, it was almost an invasion of privacy; she squirmed uncomfortably while Mum scanned the pages eagerly, admiring the stars, reading bits out, saying how *proud* Mummy was of Helen's work. She noticed that her mother was talking too loudly and too brightly; Jess and Helen, as if to balance this, were more silent than usual. Nor did it help when Mum kept looking around as if wondering where the television was. "I don't know how you manage without, Jess. It's like the Dark Ages, down here."

Helen went up to bed at nine sharp, although her bedtime had been gradually inching further and further forward. Sleep was impossible; she felt tightly strung, affected by the something-not-quite-right tension, and lay on her back, gazing at the ceiling. Her window was wide open to let in air; the heatwave had not abated. Downstairs, directly below, the kitchen window was open too, for the same reason, and it was in this way that Helen heard Mum's voice, clear and high, and Jess's, sounding much more distant, floating up ghostlike through the night.

"She's completely altered, she's like a stranger. We were always so *close*."

Then Jess, only partly audible: "... greatly improved ... scared of her own shadow ... growing up a lot ..."

"Yes, but she's so *distant*. You wouldn't understand, not being a mother—Jess, I hate to say this, but I can't help feeling that you must have been saying things to her, criticising me ..."

"... so ridiculous ... can see for yourself ..."

"I suppose not, but it's so upsetting. And she's become so rough ... dangerous games ... she should have known I wouldn't allow it. People have always said what a beautifully brought-up child she was, a perfect little lady. Now look at her. Ravines!"

"... occasional scratch won't kill her ... I wouldn't let her ... much tougher ... learning to stand up for herself."

"Jess, I don't suppose you'll ever see eye to eye with me about this ..." The voices faded as somebody pushed the window closed. Helen lay rigid, scarcely believing. She knew, now. She knew why they saw Aunt Jess so seldom. Why the atmosphere was so strained, why Mum was edgy and over-talkative, why Jess was so quiet. Why Mum rarely mentioned Jess's name, why Jess hadn't said more than the bare minimum about Mum. She had thought that something dramatic had happened long ago in the past; that one had done something unforgivable to the other. But it was much simpler than that.

Mum and Aunt Jess couldn't stand each other.

It was clear, now, seeing them together, knowing Jess as she had come to know her. They were worlds apart: diametric opposites. Jess was cool, reserved, matter-of-fact, orderly; Mum was untidy, always talking, excitable, emotional. Jess liked solitude and quiet; Mum needed people and goings-on. One had chosen to live in West Haysham, the other in Wimbledon. They had *nothing* in common. They must have driven each other crazy. But, to Helen, the most important difference had been underlined by every word she had just overheard. Jess treated her like an adult. Mum didn't even treat her as a thirteen-year-old. To her mother, she might still have been a baby. Mum wanted her to be a little lady, Mummy's darling girl of whom she was so proud. Jess wanted her to be Helen. And the two were not the same thing.

She rolled over and burrowed deeper into the bed, as if needing its comfort under the weight of her new discoveries. Because there was something very disturbing underlying all this. Given the choice between the two of them, Helen liked Jess better.

It was like breaking the law. The Commandments told you to honour your mother and father, but said nothing about aunts; she was being wicked and disloyal. But there was no getting away from it. Now the initial joy of reunion had passed, Mum, seen side by side with Jess after a separation of two months, seemed almost *silly*, at times. Oh *Lord*, she felt guilty. But was it any different from the way Mum felt about Jess? Jess had worked in that bank for eight years, and brought Mum up, more or less, but that hadn't made Mum like her. Of course, Helen still liked her mother—*loved* her—if only she wouldn't talk in that baby way. "Mummy's tired" . . . She simply didn't *want* to be a perfect little lady. She didn't *want* to be called 'darling' with every other breath.

But she couldn't show this. She would have to be squeezed and hugged, fussed over and babied, and take it all smiling. Otherwise there would be no end of trouble. Mum would get at Aunt Jess and say awful things about what Jess had done to her while Mum was away. Helen felt fiercely protective of Aunt Jess. But Mum would never understand this. She sighed, gustily. If this was growing up, it certainly made life more complicated.

She rolled over again, knowing that sleep was still a long way off.

It was peculiar, seeing the two of them chatting over their coffee cups the next morning. Helen's imagination had built things up until she half-expected them to be glaring in hostile silence, or hitting each other with saucepans. But Jess looked up, smiled and said: "Don't tell me, let me guess. Shredded Wheat" and Helen said: "Right." Mum, who had not been up in time to watch the Cereal Rotation System in action the day before, glanced at her in surprise, but made no comment. It was just another day, but it wasn't the same. She knew too much. She couldn't watch Jess, or Mum, without picturing the same scene fifteen years ago, herself non-existent, Jess steeling herself for another day at Barclays, Mum longing to get away. It was creepy. Were they thinking the same thing?

Jess suggested that Mum might go into Stambury on the bus. "There's usually one along between ten and eleven."

"I don't see myself standing around for an hour waiting for a *possible* bus—you're so cut off, here, Jess, it's scarcely believable." The charms of West Haysham were rapidly wearing thin. At first it had been 'so picturesque, so peaceful'; then this had subtly changed to 'quiet as the grave'. It could only be a matter of time before it was the back of beyond and the last place on God's earth, both of which terms Helen had heard her mother use when describing the village to friends.

In the end, Mum only lasted four days.

'I've had enough of this place," she announced. "I'll go spare. I've rung work, and I'm starting back on Monday. I'm fit as a fiddle." Her departure was even more abrupt than her arrival; she was packed and ready to leave within an hour, as if the combination of Jess, the back of beyond and a changed Helen was all too much for her.

"Mummy's going to miss you terribly," she told Helen, almost in tears, while the taxi-driver waited patiently outside. "Be a good girl—it's only for ten days now, and you'll be home." Then another violent squeeze, and she was gone. Helen went out and watched the taxi until it was out of sight, waving, but her mother didn't turn round once, which could mean either of two things; she might actually be crying, or it could be a reproach to Helen, for not being the same. For growing up.

Suddenly she felt tired of all these highly-charged adult emotions, most of which seemed so unnecessary, and, whirling round, went back indoors to get on with her new editorial.

Chapter Thirteen

—≈ ❋ ❋ ≈—

JESS LOOKED DRAINED. She was stroking Logan, talking to him softly with the expression of one who on occasion finds animals a great deal saner than human beings.

"An Editor's work is never done," she remarked, watching Helen write. "How's it going?"

"I've had a new idea. You know in your *Telegraph*, where it says Court Circular, there's a list of people with birthdays? I'm going to print everyone who's got a birthday this month. They'll like that."

"They will indeed. Why not go the whole hog and do Lists of Engagements? You know, as in 'Princess Margaret is launching a boot factory in Bognor at 2.30'. It would be scintillating stuff. Michael Pargeter will be attending the dentist at 4.15 on Friday . . ."

Things were back to normal. The tension had gone from the house as surely as if her mother had packed it in her case and taken it with her. Everything could change so quickly. Helen realized with a sense of shock that she had actually been rather relieved to see her mother go. Mum was simply wrong here, like an Eskimo at the Equator.

"Finished your editorial?"

"Just about. It's a mixture of things this time, saying

what a success Issue One was, and thanking everyone for their support, and that the Editor's very sorry but she has to quit, so That's All Folks ... not nearly so good as last month's. Aunt Jess—you would know by now, wouldn't you? I mean about the school getting the chop ..."

"Yes, thank heavens, it does seem to have fizzled out. Another false alarm. So we're safe for the time being. Till the next time."

"And you think the editorial helped?"

"The editorial—oh, Helen! Did I give you the impression ... that inspector wasn't anything to do with that! Everyone gets them. Routine. Oh, don't look so disappointed! I should have realised—the propaganda—never mind. It was very good propaganda."

"But it was wasted."

"Not at all. Who's to know who passes the word, tips the wink, nudge nudge? You may have helped. Certainly you didn't do any harm."

This was small consolation, but perhaps saving the school singlehanded had been a *bit* ambitious. Anyway, he *had* read it, and *might* have tipped the wink and nudge nudged. As Jess said, who was to know?

"Not long now," said Mrs. Page, in high good humour. "Pennines, moors, no heathen Southerners ..."

"Aaah, she loves us really," said Joanne. The top group were not gripped by end-of-term fever to quite the same extent as the rest. Except for Helen, they had been at West Haysham School for as long as they could remember, and had watched the annual departure of other top groups, bound for the Chase, never to return; now it was their turn, and they weren't at all sure that they liked it.

"You'll have to disband your harem, Paul," said Mrs. Page. "After all these years."

"*Horrible* women," said Paul, but he too had a faint air of apprehension under the habitual wry expression. "They're coming too, aren't they. I can't get away from them. They'll follow me to the grave."

"Ah, well. That's life."

"With Esther Rancid," chanted everyone within earshot.

"And this week's talented pet," said Paul, glad of the change of subject. "A trampolining goldfish from Liverpool."

"Sometimes I wonder why I ever became a teacher," Mrs. Page said. "In my next reincarnation I'll follow my instincts and be an engine driver."

"In your next reincarnation you might be a trampolining goldfish from Liverpool," said Paul, correctly judging that he would get away with this on his very last day. Mrs. Page tapped him mildly on the head with a book, produced six tubes of Smarties and handed them round.

"With all our compliments, in the hope that you will carry the fine traditions of West Haysham to your new school, etcetera etcetera. And ruin your teeth and your beautiful waistlines."

"We'll be a bigger form next year," someone said.

"Let's see. Six leaving. Who's coming up? Daniel, Emma . . ."

"Michael Pargeter," said Andrew Pargeter.

"Don't remind me. Three Pargeters in one form. I think I'll take a correspondence course in engine driving during the holidays."

Helen and Melanie walked home together, cardigans slung over shoulders, eating Smarties. The colours ran in the heat, giving them sticky fingers and Smartie-coloured hands.

"Someone's doctored this," Helen said, emptying her tube into her hand for inspection. "Only four orange ones. It's a conspiracy."

"You know, it's an awful shame you can't stay for the summer. You don't really *have* to go back till September, do you?"

"No, but ..." That was a thought. She didn't. With Mum back at work and the flat empty all day, surely it would be far more practical for her to stay here with Jess; a summer in the country, a summer of playing fields and Melanie and seaside with the Pargeters ... "Of course! Why on earth didn't I think of that? I'll fix it straight away." She whacked Melanie on the back in congratulation, leaving a multi-coloured patch on the white dress which nearly gave Mrs. Davies a fit.

"Absolutely not," said Jess.

It was like a physical blow.

"But it would be so much better—Mum's working— and unless you'd rather I wasn't ..." she faltered.

"Of course I'd like you to stay, birdbrain. But think of your mother for a moment. Not long recovered from a hysterectomy, working all day in a hot office, coming home to an empty flat—Barbara isn't good at being alone. She needs you there. And while I'm quite extraordinarily fond of you, I don't need you."

Helen said nothing.

"Helen, you've been apart for nearly three months! She's your mother. She wants you back."

"She's changed, though. She was different. Didn't you think so?"

"Only the hairstyle. Not otherwise. It's you that's changed, I told you that. You've grown up three years in that many months."

"Yes, but she didn't like it. I'll have to change back, or there'll be trouble. I know there will."

"You can't change back. Nobody can decide to un-grow up. Anyhow, you're still basically the same person, just a little older and wiser, a few improvements here and there. Which version of yourself do *you* prefer?"

"I'd rather be like I am now. But didn't you think . . . the way she talked to me . . . ."

"Just the same as always, I assure you. In fact, you used to say the same sort of things, in reverse, if you see what I mean." Jess didn't actually *say* 'and I used to think you were as soft as she was' but the implication was there. "What you have to do is to go back and show your mother, gradually, that the alterations have been for the better. Once she gets used to it she'll prefer you as you are now. I certainly do."

Helen doubted that it would be as simple as that. Oh, well.

"I suppose there'll be Deborah."

"Of course. Come on, cheer up, holidays are upon us and you're looking like the back of a hearse. You know— even if I asked, Barbara wouldn't let you stay here for the summer. She nearly took you with her when she left last week."

"*Did* she?"

"She did. So there's no point in brooding over ifs and might-have-beens, because there aren't any. Tell you what, I'll give you my farewell present a little early. It's something I . . ."

"No, don't tell me. Can I guess?"

"Surely."

"*Suzy Mucks Out.*"

"You're very close."

"Sherrilyn Comfort."

110

"Damn, you've cracked it." Jess hit her head with her fist. "O.K., Sherrilyn, you can come out of the fridge. The game's up."

Helen spluttered. "Give up." Jess passed her a parcel, wrapped in blue paper, small, hard, light . . . she shook it, thought she detected a faint rattle. "Have I seen one before?"

"You've seen *that* one before. Often." Bemused, Helen ripped it open. It was *The War of the Worlds*.

"Aunt Jess, you can't . . . this is *valuable*."

"Not to me it's not. If I hear it once more I'll go bananas. Already I'm imagining I hear Red Weed creeping up the path in the night. It's yours, with my deepest gratitude for livening my summer up. Now, if you want to be at the Pargeters' in time for Blue Peter, you'd better be on your way."

"Will you carry on with this next year?" she asked Richard, as they flicked idly through the pages of Issue Two.

"I hope so. I know Mrs. Page wants to keep it on. Can't think who to have for assistant, though. Andrew would be best, but I can't do that or they'll start talking about another Pargeter takeover."

"Do people really say things like that?"

"All the time."

Michael zoomed past the window, wearing very little, making a throaty yodelling noise.

"It's a Tarzan day," said his mother, coming in with iced drinks. "Don't volunteer to be Jane, Helen, I couldn't guarantee your safety." Helen grinned, taking a glass. She found it very difficult to keep her eyes off Mrs. Pargeter's middle. There was a fatal attraction in the very fact that you oughtn't to stare.

"You'll have to start a Births, Marriages and Deaths column," she said. "For Elizabeth Louise."

"We don't get that many marriages in school. Though we might if Sherrilyn Comfort had anything to do with it. Hold on, anyway. The baby may have decided to be Christopher Matthew. I'll believe in Elizabeth Louise when I see her."

"I'll never see her at all," Helen said sadly.

"Of course you will. Next year." Helen looked blank. "You'll have to come back, to hand the trophy over to the next winner."

"Oh, yes! I never thought of that. That'll be you, too, the next winner."

"Probably," agreed Richard. "I dare say we'll be quite pleased to see you. You're not so bad. Not now. At first you were a washout."

"Thanks a *million* ... Oh, well, all that rain, it was enough to wash anybody out. Everything turned upside down, half-way. You didn't turn out to be such a bad sandwich filling, Richard Pargeter."

It had been a most peculiar sandwich. One half had been not only fish paste, but fish paste mixed with cold gravy, semolina, dead slug and washing-up liquid. But the second half had been something else altogether; not even peanut butter, better than that. So delicious that if she knew the recipe she'd be an overnight millionaire.

Richard's face was creased in perplexity, but she just smiled, and lowered her eyes to the magazine.